Notebook WRITER'S GUIDE

 **Children's Publishing**

Published by American Education Publishing, an imprint of McGraw-Hill Children's Publishing, A Division of The McGraw-Hill Companies.

Printed in the United States of America.

Send all inquiries to:
McGraw-Hill Children's Publishing
8787 Orion Place
Columbus, Ohio 43240-4027

ISBN 1-57768-646-2

1 2 3 4 5 6 7 8 9 10 MAL 08 07 06 05 04 03

TABLE OF CONTENTS

SECTION I
GRAMMAR

In the following section you will find a grammar guide explaining each of the eight parts of speech. Keep reading to learn how to identify and use the parts of speech correctly. Knowing grammar will help you to improve every part of your writing.

THE EIGHT PARTS OF SPEECH

Parts of speech are categories of words. The categories are based on how words are used in a sentence. Many words can fit into more than one category. For example, *round* can be an adjective, noun, verb, adverb, or preposition.

> A marble is *round*.
> We sang a *round*.
> *Round* these numbers to the nearest tenth.
> Gather *round*.
> The worried parents waited *round* the telephone.

In English, there are eight parts of speech.

1. NOUNS name a person, place, thing, or idea.
> child, James, school, tree, courage

2. PRONOUNS take the place of nouns.
> they, me, hers, herself, who, those

3. VERBS show action or a state of being.
> tackle, think, am, was

4. ADJECTIVES describe a noun or pronoun.
> shiny, happier, best

5. ADVERBS modify a verb, an adjective, or another adverb.
> well, carefully, very

6. PREPOSITIONS show the position or relationship between a noun and another word.
> over, from, in spite of

7. CONJUNCTIONS connect words or phrases.
> and, yet, but, or, neither/nor

8. INTERJECTIONS show emotion.
> Ouch! Yikes! Hooray!

NOUNS

A **noun** names a person, a place, a thing, or an idea. There are several different types of nouns.

Singular and Plural Nouns

A **singular noun** names one person, place, or thing.

>   boy, park, swing

A **plural noun** names more than one person, place, or thing.

>   cups, plates, bowls

Plural Noun Rules

- To change most singular nouns to plural nouns, add *s*.
    > cups, bowls
- To nouns ending in *s*, *ch*, *sh*, or *x*, add *es*.
    > buses, peaches, dishes, taxes
- To nouns ending in *y* after a vowel, add *s*.
    > days, keys
- To nouns ending in *y* after a consonant, change the *y* to *i* and add *es*.
    > parties, flies
- To nouns ending in *o* after a vowel, add *s*.
    > rodeos, radios
- To nouns ending in *o* after a consonant, add *es*.
    > potatoes, tomatoes
- Words that refer to music are exceptions.
    > pianos, solos
- To some nouns ending in *f* or *fe*, change the *f* or *fe* to *ves*. You need to memorize or look up which nouns to change.
    > safes, knives, roofs, leaves
- Some nouns, including many animals, have irregular plurals.
    > children, feet, mice, deer

Common and Proper Nouns

A **common noun** is a word that names any person, place, or thing. Common nouns do not begin with a capital letter unless they are the first word of a sentence.

>   river, country, boy, girl, dog, school

A **proper noun** is a word that names a special person, place, or thing. Proper nouns begin with a capital letter.

>   Ohio River, Mexico, Danny, Amy, Spot, Center Middle School

Abstract and Concrete Nouns

An **abstract noun** names an idea, quality, or state of mind.

>   peace, patience, success, sadness

A **concrete noun** names something that can be seen or touched.

>   road, flower, house, animal, Joe

Possessive Nouns

A **possessive noun** shows ownership. It tells who or what owns something. To make a singular noun show possession or ownership, add an apostrophe and an *s*.

Jason—Jason's ball
Carla—Carla's dress
Maggie—Maggie's book

To make a plural noun show possession or ownership, add an apostrophe after the final *s*.

girls—girls' basketballs
parks—parks' benches

If the plural noun does not end in *s*, add an apostrophe and an *s* as you would for a singular noun.

children—children's
men—men's

Collective Nouns

A **collective noun** names a group of people, places, or things. When a collective noun refers to a group as a unit, it is considered singular. When it refers to the individual members of the group that are acting separately, it is considered plural.

singular collective nouns:
The *school* of fish lives in the cool water.
Our *team* usually wins.
plural collective nouns:
The *school* of fish are all swimming in different directions.
The *team* are all expected to earn good grades.

Some common collective nouns are: *assortment, gang, collection, crowd, group, herd, crew, band, batch, pile, set, troop, bunch, team, pride of lions, gaggle of geese, school of fish, murder of crows, swarm of bees, pack of dogs, flock of sheep.*

Predicate Nouns

A **predicate noun** is a noun that comes after a linking verb and refers back to the subject. It is used as a subject complement. (The subject of the sentence and the predicate noun represent the same thing.)

Leo was the fiercest *lion* in the zoo.

Noun Clauses

A **noun clause** is a dependent clause that functions as a noun. It may be used as a subject, a direct object, an indirect object, an object of a preposition, or a predicate noun.

subject: *What occurred* was not planned at all.
direct object: They wondered *what they should do* now.
indirect object: Should they make *whoever broke the window* pay the bill?
object of the preposition: They were grateful to *whomever cleaned up the mess.*
predicate noun: The good thing was *that no one was hurt.*

Appositives

An **appositive** is a noun or noun phrase placed next to or very near another noun or noun phrase. It identifies, explains, or adds to its meaning or renames the initial noun or pronoun.

Bones, *the scaffolding of the body*, are tied together with ligaments.

PRONOUNS

A **pronoun** takes the place of a noun. Every pronoun has an **antecedent**. An antecedent is the noun that a pronoun refers to or replaces. A pronoun must agree with its antecedent in number, person, and gender.

> *Juan* shined his shoes after *he* walked through the mud.
> The *girls* are baking the cake *they* promised to make for the fundraiser.

When a singular pronoun is followed by another pronoun, the second pronoun must also be singular. The following are all singular pronouns:

someone	anyone	everyone	none	each
somebody	anybody	everybody	nobody	everything

> **Incorrect:** Everybody has finished *their* assignment.
> **Correct:** Everybody has finished *his* or *her* assignment.
> **Incorrect:** Has anyone finished *their* dinner?
> **Correct:** Has anyone finished *his* or *her* dinner?

Personal Pronouns
Personal pronouns name the speaker, the person spoken to, or the person or thing spoken about. They are:

singular: I, my, mine, he, his, him,
      she, her, hers, it, its
      you, your, yours

plural: we, our, ours, us
      you, your, yours
      they, them, their, theirs

Relative Pronouns
The pronouns *that, which,* and *who* are called **relative pronouns**.
Use *who* when speaking of people.

> The girl *who* arrived is my sister.

Use *which* when including extra information about animals or things that is not needed to understand the sentence. Set off these *which* phrases with commas.

> His dog, *which* is a Dalmatian, has won many awards.

Use *that* when speaking of people, things, or animals.

> The house *that* we live in is painted blue.

Subject Pronouns
Use a **subject pronoun** (*I, you, he, she, it, we, they*) when the pronoun is the subject of a sentence or clause.

> *He* said Aunt Ellen would come at 2:00.
> *They* were worried when *she* didn't come.

Pronouns that follow the verb *be* restate the subject, so they need to be subject pronouns.

> "Who is *it*?" asked the Third Little Pig.
> "It is *I*!" snarled the Big Bad Wolf.
> "It is *he*!" gasped the other two pigs.

Object Pronouns
Use an **object pronoun** (me, you, him, her, it, us, them) when the pronoun directly

receives the action of a verb.

Aunt Ellen called *them* later.

Use an object pronoun when the pronoun indirectly receives the action of a verb.

Aunt Ellen sent *us* flowers.

Use an object pronoun when the pronoun is the object of a preposition.

Uncle Charlie took a picture of *her*.

Intensive Pronouns

An **intensive pronoun** emphasizes, or intensifies, the noun or pronoun it refers to. An intensive pronoun can be omitted. It is optional.

The children *themselves* designed this playground.

The owner *himself* took us on the tour.

Reflexive Pronouns

A **reflexive pronoun** refers the action back to the noun or pronoun. A reflexive pronoun is not optional. Omitting it changes the meaning or makes the sentence incomplete.

She reminded *herself* not to mention the surprise party.

Possessive Pronouns

A **possessive pronoun** is one that shows ownership or possession. Possessive pronouns include *my, mine, your, yours, his, her, its, our, ours, their, theirs*.

He forgot *his* homework as he raced out of school.

Indefinite Pronouns

An **indefinite pronoun** is one that refers generally, not specifically, to people, places, or things. Some indefinite pronouns are always singular, some are always plural, and some may be either singular or plural.

singular indefinite pronouns: *anyone, everyone, no one, someone, something*
plural indefinite pronouns: *many, both, few, several, others*
singular or plural indefinite pronouns: *all, any, most, some, none*

Predicate Pronouns

A **subject complement** is a word that comes after a linking verb and refers back to the subject. When a pronoun is used, it is called a **predicate pronoun**.

That flashlight is *hers*.

Interrogative Pronouns

An **interrogative pronoun** introduces a question. *Who, what, which, when, how,* and *why* are common interrogative pronouns.

What event does Becky plan to enter?
Which school will Manuel choose?

Demonstrative Pronouns

A **demonstrative pronoun** shows, or demonstrates, which noun is being talked about in the sentence. *That, these, this,* and *those* are demonstrative pronouns. Be careful! Because these four words can also be adjectives, a demonstrative pronoun has to take the place of a specific noun.

demonstrative pronoun: Please load *this* and *that* onto the truck.
adjective: *Those* shoes are too dirty for you to come in *this* house.

VERBS

All **verbs** help make a statement. Most verbs help make a statement by showing action.
> Jack *cooked* dinner.

Verbs can also show a state of being.
> She *looks* worried.

Action Verbs

An **action verb** shows action. It shows what someone or something does, did, or will do.
> Grandmother and I *baked* a cake.
> Cheryl *plays* softball every afternoon.

Linking Verbs

Other verbs help show the appearance or condition of something. These verbs are called **linking verbs**. Linking verbs connect, or link, the subject of the sentence to a word or words in the predicate.
> Her dress *is* lovely.

The verb *to be* is the most common linking verb.

> present: I am, we are   past: I was, we were
> you are   you were
> he is, she is, it is, they are   he was, she was, it was, they were

Any verb that can be substituted by a form of *to be* is a linking verb. Other common linking verbs are: *seem, become, appear, remain, look,* and *feel*.

Helping Verbs

Sometimes a sentence needs more than one verb to make the statement clear. These words are called **helping verbs**.
> common helping verbs: *am, are, is, was, were, do, did, have, has, had, can, may*

A **verb phrase** contains one or more helping verbs along with the main verb.
> Terry *had drawn* a beautiful picture.
> William *must have worn* an overcoat.
> *Were* the children *walking* to school?

Transitive and Intransitive Verbs

A **transitive verb** is an action verb that is followed by a direct object. The verb "transmits" the action from the subject to the object.

An **intransitive verb** does not need an object to complete its meaning. It is often followed by a prepositional phrase.
> transitive: We *caught* a fish.
> intransitive: I *fish* with my dad.

Infinitives

An **infinitive** is a present tense verb that follows the word *to* (to + verb = infinitive). An infinitive can act as a noun, an adjective, or an adverb.
> George sat on the front step *to finish* his ice-cream cone.

An **infinitive phrase** includes modifiers, a complement, or a subject, which act together as a single part of speech.

    subject: *To make dinner* for Grandma was Lesley's reason for taking a cooking class.

    predicate noun: Lesley's hope is *to make a seven-course meal.*

Gerunds

A **gerund** is a verb form ending in *ing* that functions as a noun. Adding *ing* to a verb in the present tense forms a gerund. A **gerund phrase** is a group of words that includes a gerund and its related words.

    gerund: *Dancing* is my favorite form of exercise.

    gerund phrase: *Dancing the polka* is a good workout.

Participles

A **participle** is a verb form that can function as an adjective. Adding *ing* to a present tense verb usually forms the present participle. The past participle is usually formed by adding *ed* to the present tense. A **participial phrase** is a group of words that includes the participle and its objects, complements, or modifiers.

    present participle: Rex barks at the *passing* cars.

    past participle: A *determined* Rex tried to chase the car.

Verb Tense

Verb tense shows the time in which the action takes place. There are six tenses: present, past, future, present perfect, past perfect, and future perfect.

Present tense shows action or a state of being that is happening now.

    I *eat* chocolate.

Past tense shows an action or state of being that has been completed.

    I *ate* chocolate.

Future tense shows action or a state of being that will take place. The helping verb *will* is usually used with the principal verb to form the future tense.

    I *will eat* chocolate.

The **present-perfect tense** is formed using the present tense of the helping verb *to have* plus the past tense of the verb it helps. This combination is called the **past participle**. Together, the tense they form is called the present-perfect tense.

    has (present tense of helping verb) + past participle action verb = present-perfect tense

    Our cousins *have arrived* at last.

The past tense of an action verb shows a definite time something happened in the past. The present-perfect tense shows an indefinite time when something happened and shows that it may still be going on.

    The cruise ship *arrived* late. (definite: *Late* answers when it arrived.)

    The cruise ship *has arrived*. (indefinite: *It* has arrived at some time.)

Because the two tenses are used to show a definite or indefinite action, you should be careful when mixing the two tenses.

    Correct: My dad told me to clean my room yesterday.

        (*Yesterday* is a definite time.)

    Incorrect: My dad *has told* me to clean my room yesterday.

        (*Has told* cannot be used to show a definite time, and *yesterday* is definite.)

The **past-perfect tense** is formed using the past tense of the verb *to have* plus the past participle.

> had (past tense of helping verb) + past participle action verb = past-perfect tense

When talking about things that have happened in the past, use the past-perfect tense to show which action happened first.

> Mike *went* to the restaurant.
> His friends *talked* about the restaurant.

Did the friends tell Mike that the restaurant was good before or after he went to the restaurant? Using the past-perfect tense shows which action happened first.

> His friends *talked* about the restaurant.
> Mike *had gone* to the restaurant.

The **future-perfect tense** is formed using the verbs *will* and *have* plus the past participle.

> will (auxiliary verb) + have (helping verb) + past participle = future perfect tense

Use the future-perfect tense to show the "future past." When talking about things that will happen in the future, the future-perfect tense shows that an action will be completed before another.

> My science project *is* due on Monday during fourth period.
> I *will have finished* the project by then.

In this example, the future-perfect tense shows that the project will be finished before it is due. The events will happen in the future, but one will happen first. This is the "future past."

Active and Passive Voice

A verb is in the **active voice** when the subject is performing the action.

> Mike *ate* the last piece of cake.

A verb is in the **passive voice** when the subject receives the action or is the result of the action.

> The last piece of cake *was eaten* by Mike.

Tip: Change sentences in passive voice to active voice whenever possible. Active voice is much stronger than passive voice, and using active voice will make your writing clearer and more exciting.

Subject–Verb Agreement Rules

One of the most important parts of writing sentences is making a subject and its verb agree. Most of us can tell the difference between which verb to use (*like* or *likes*) in a simple sentence such as this: Jose *likes* to draw. Sentences with compound subjects, tricky pronouns, or collective nouns are more difficult. Here are some guidelines to help you.

- Singular subjects use singular verbs. Plural subjects use plural verbs.
  > Jen *likes* chicken.
  > All the kids *like* chicken.
- Compound subjects connected by *and* use a plural verb.
  > Mike and Karen *play* soccer.
- Compound subjects connected by *or* use a singular verb if the subject following *or* is singular and a plural verb if the subject following *or* is plural.
  > Who knows where or when it *will rain*.
  > How or why they *changed* the show I don't know.

- Most indefinite pronouns are singular and require a singular verb.
  anyone, anything, each, either, everybody, everyone, everything, neither, no one, nothing, one, someone, something
- Some indefinite pronouns can be singular or plural depending on the use.
  both, few, many, others, several
- Most collective nouns require a singular verb because the group acts as one.
  audience, bunch, class, family, group, herd, pack, set, team
- If a group is divided and its members are acting as individuals, it may use a plural noun.

Irregular Verbs

Irregular verbs form their tenses by a change in spelling or word form. The only way to know irregular verbs is to use and memorize them. Most verbs follow the regular rules. There are only about 50 irregular verbs. Some of them are:

be	do	go	run	teach
become	draw	grow	say	tear
begin	drink	know	see	think
blow	drive	lay (put down)	set	throw
break	eat	lead (guide)	shake	wear
burn	fight	lend	sing	write
burst	fly	lie (recline)	speak	
choose	forget	lie (tell a lie)	steal	
come	freeze	lose	strike	
dive	get	rise	swim	

ADJECTIVES

An **adjective** is a word that describes a noun or pronoun in three ways.
An adjective tells **what kind**.

>The *fluffy* yellow duckling looked for its mother.

An adjective tells **which one**.

>*That* boy is in my class this year.

An adjective tells **how many**.

>I'll give you *several* reasons why you must write two reports.

Positive, Comparative, and Superlative Adjectives

Some adjectives are used to compare nouns. The **positive adjective** describes a noun or pronoun without comparing it to anyone or anything else. A **comparative adjective** is used to describe a comparison between two things, people, places, or actions. A **superlative adjective** compares three or more things, people, places, or actions.

	positive	comparative	superlative
adjectives	happy	happier	happiest
	good	better	best

Demonstrative Adjectives

This, that, these, and *those* are **demonstrative adjectives** that modify nouns by telling "which one" or "which ones." *This* and *that* are singular. *These* and *those* are plural. *This* and *these* refer to things nearby, and *that* and *those* refer to things farther away.

>*This* zoo we are visiting is the best in the state.
>*That* zoo across town isn't nearly as nice.
>*These* animals we are seeing are cared for very well.
>*Those* animals over there are not cared for as well.

Indefinite Adjectives

An **indefinite adjective** is an adjective that gives an estimated number or quantity or that refers to no specific person or thing. It does not tell exactly how many or how much.

>When we go out, we bring a *few* snacks to share with each other.

Articles

A, an, and *the* are special adjectives called **articles**. They are used to describe a singular noun. The word *a* is used before a word that begins with a consonant sound, and the word *an* is used before a word that begins with a vowel sound.

>*A* bunny is nesting under *the* porch.
>*The* baby bunnies are eating up *the* garden.

Predicate Adjectives

A **subject complement** is a word that comes after a linking verb and refers back to the subject. An adjective used as a subject complement is called a predicate adjective. A **predicate adjective** follows a linking verb and describes the subject.

>Laura's flashlight is *bright*.

ADVERBS

An **adverb** is a word that usually describes a verb. It can also describe an adjective or another adverb.

An adverb tells **how**.
> The boy ran *fast*.

An adverb tells **when**.
> Dinner will be ready at *five o'clock*.

An adverb tells **where**.
> Joshua played *nearby*.

An adverb tells **how often**.
> Julie takes dance lessons *daily*.

Positive, Comparative, and Superlative Adverbs

Adverbs, like adjectives, have three degrees of comparison. The **positive adverb** describes a noun, pronoun, or adjective without comparing it to anyone or anything else. A **comparative adverb** is used to describe a comparison between two things, people, places, or actions. A **superlative adverb** compares three or more things, people, places, or actions. Some adverbs form the comparative degree by adding *er* and the superlative degree by adding *est*. Most adverbs that end in *ly* form their comparative degrees by adding the words *more* or *less* in front of the positive degree. Adding the words *most* or *least* in front of the positive degree forms the superlative.

> Raquel danced *less gracefully* than her sisters.
> I hope they will come *sooner* rather than *later*.

	positive	comparatives	superlatives
adverbs	happily	more/less happily	most/least happily
	well	better	best
	fast	faster	fastest

Adverb Clauses

An **adverb clause** is a dependent clause that functions as an adverb. It can modify verbs, adjectives, or other adverbs and tells *where, when, in what manner, to what extent, under what condition,* or *why*.

> We dress warmly *when we play in the snow*.

Qualifying Adverbs

Adverbs can modify other adverbs. These adverbs are called **qualifying adverbs**. They strengthen or weaken the adverbs they modify. They answer the questions *how much* or *to what extent*.

> He walked on the ice *very carefully*.
> (*Very* strengthens the adverb *carefully*.)
> No one on the field trip knew *quite exactly* where to find the bus.
> (*Quite* weakens the adverb *exactly*.)

PREPOSITIONS

A **preposition** is a connecting word. It connects ideas. A preposition also shows the relationship between a noun or pronoun and some other word or idea in the sentence.

A preposition shows **time**.
> *before, after, during, until, while, since*

A preposition shows **direction**.
> *across, toward, from, around, behind*

A preposition shows **cause**.
> *on account of, in spite of, due to, because of, since*

A preposition shows **position**.
> *above, against, beneath, on, over, under, inside*

Prepositional Phrases

A **prepositional phrase** is a group of words starting with a preposition. The phrase usually ends with a noun or pronoun. It can function as an adjective or an adverb, depending on the word it modifies. Like a one-word adjective, an adjective prepositional phrase modifies only a noun or a pronoun.

> I heard the news *on the radio*.
> Rita reached *into the bag*.

A sentence may have more than one prepositional phrase.

> I listened *to the news* *on* the radio.
> Rita reached *into* the bag *for* an apple.

Like a one-word adverb, an adverb prepositional phrase usually modifies a verb and may tell where, how, or when an action takes place.

> The White House is located *in Washington, DC*. (tells where)
> The president resides there *with his family members*. (tells how)
> He will leave the White House *at the end of his term*. (tells when)

Object of the Proposition

The noun or pronoun used as the **object of the preposition** follows the preposition or prepositional phrase. A preposition relates the noun or pronoun to another word in the sentence.

Introductory Phrases

Many **introductory phrases** and clauses begin with a preposition. Use a comma to separate these phrases from the rest of the sentence.

> *Because* I am sick, I will not be able to go on the field trip.

List of Prepositions

aboard	considering	from between	in regard to	outside
alongside	despite	from under	inside	over to
away from	down from	in addition to	instead of	regarding
behind	except for	in front of	on account of	underneath
besides	from among	in place of	on behalf of	within

CONJUNCTIONS

Conjunctions are connecting words. They can connect words, phrases, or sentences. *And, or, but, for,* and *yet* are all conjunctions. Use conjunctions to combine subjects, predicates, or two smaller, related sentences. This helps your writing to flow more smoothly.

    Compound subject:
        Cindy is learning to surf. I am learning to surf.
        Cindy *and* I are learning to surf.
    Compound predicate:
        Cindy likes to surf. Cindy likes to skateboard.
        Cindy likes to surf *and* skateboard.
    Compound sentences:
        Cindy likes to surf. She is getting better at it.
        Cindy likes to surf, *and* she is getting better at it.

Coordinating and Subordinating Conjunctions

Conjunctions are words that join words or groups of words. *And, but, or, nor,* and *for* are **coordinating conjunctions** because they coordinate, or organize, the connection between two independent clauses.

    Becky lives down the street, *and* we're going to her house after school.

Subordinating conjunctions show the connection between a dependent, or subordinating clause, and the rest of the sentence. *As, when, because, since, unless,* and *before* can be subordinating conjunctions. When the subordinating clause comes at the beginning of the sentence, a comma follows it.

    I will iron. You are tired.
    I will iron *whenever* you are tired.
    Because you are tired, I will iron.

INTERJECTIONS

An **interjection** is a word that shows strong feeling.

    Ouch! That really hurt!

Sometimes an interjection is a short phrase.

    You're kidding! I would never go in that cave by myself.

An interjection begins with a capital letter, ends in an exclamation point, and is separate from a sentence.

    Yikes!

Some words that are used as interjections are also used in sentences to show mild feeling. These are called **mild interjections**. When used this way, they are followed by a comma, not an exclamation point.

    Oh, whoops, I dropped my books.

List of Interjections

Ouch!	Great!	Yes!	Please!	Not on your life!
Oh!	Well!	No!	Watch out!	Alright!
Aha!	Oh no!	Hurrah!	Of course!	Awesome!

SECTION 2
USAGE

Usage is how we use language correctly and properly. Although many neighborhoods and groups have their own patterns of informal speech, it is important that all students learn to speak and write standard English. Standard English is the language of educated people. Many people judge others by the way they speak. What would your initial reaction be to someone who said, "He don't know nothing"? This section on usage will help you write clear sentences, give you tips on using words correctly, and give you help with confusing pronouns.

WRITING SENTENCES WITH CLARITY

The Four Kinds of Sentences
There are four kinds of sentences.
A **declarative** sentence makes a statement. It should end in a period.
> Karen plays basketball.

An **imperative** sentence gives a command. It should end in a period.
> Karen, come here.

An **interrogative** sentence asks a question. It should end in a question mark.
> Where is Karen?

An **exclamatory** sentence shows surprise or strong emotion. It should end in an exclamation point.
> Karen's team won!

Clauses
An **independent clause** is a group of words with a subject and a predicate that states a complete thought and can stand by itself as a sentence. A **dependent clause** cannot stand alone. It depends on the independent clause of the sentence to complete its meaning. Dependent clauses start with words like *who, which, that, because, when, if, until, before,* and *after.*

> *When* we went to the school carnival, we saw lots of clowns.
> (dependent)   (independent)

Fragments and Run-ons
Groups of words that do not tell or ask us something are called sentence **fragments**.
> fragment: the blue cup
> complete sentence: Randy drank cocoa from the blue cup.

Run-on sentences usually occur when end punctuation is left out of sentences. Always remember to put end punctuation at the end of a sentence.
> run-on: It was Donna's turn to bat she hit a home run what a sight!
> complete sentences: It was Donna's turn to bat. She hit a home run. What a sight!

Subjects and Predicates

Every sentence has two parts: the subject and the predicate. The **complete subject** consists of all the words in the sentence that describe what or who is being talked about. The **complete predicate** consists of all the words in the sentence that describe what the subject is doing, did, or will do.

> My friend, Glenda, baby-sits every Saturday.
> complete subject: My friend, Glenda
> complete predicate: baby-sits every Saturday.

Simple Subjects and Predicates

The **simple subject** is the main word in the complete subject. The **simple predicate** or predicate verb is the main verb or verb phrase in the complete predicate.

> My friend, Glenda, baby-sits every Saturday.
> simple subject: Glenda
> simple predicate: baby-sits

Compound Subjects and Predicates

A **compound subject** is made of two or more subjects that have the same verb and are joined by a conjunction such as *and* or *or*.

> The king of Spain believed in the cities of gold.
> The queen of Spain believed in the cities of gold.
> compound subject: The king and queen of Spain believed in the cities of gold.

A **compound predicate** is two or more predicates that have the same subject and are joined by a conjunction.

> The Spanish believed in a fairy tale.
> The Spanish followed the legend of the cities of gold.
> compound predicate: The Spanish believed a fairy tale and followed the legend of the cities of gold.

Both a compound subject and compound predicate can be in one sentence.

> My sister *and* I   love to make *and* eat caramel apples.
> (compound subject)   (compound predicate)

Simple, Compound, Complex, and Compound-Complex Sentences

A **simple sentence** contains one independent clause.

> Maxwell is a sumo wrestler.

A **compound sentence** contains two independent clauses that are closely related. A comma and a conjunction or a semicolon usually connects the two clauses.

> Clocks tell time. They are also used for decoration.
> compound sentence: Clocks tell time, *but* they are also used for decoration.

A **complex sentence** contains an independent clause and one or more dependent clauses. A dependent clause often begins with a relative pronoun, such as *who, which, whose, that,* or *whom.*

> The butterfly, <u>*whose* wings were brightly colored</u>, flitted from flower to flower.
>   (dependent clause)

A **compound-complex sentence** contains two or more independent clauses and at least one dependent clause.

> _When_ I get home from school, I like to eat a sandwich, and I like to listen to music.
> (dependent clause)

Modifiers

The complete subject or complete predicate of a sentence usually contains words or phrases called **modifiers** that add to the meaning of the sentence.

> The ancient tombs, _which stand powerfully on the hot sands of Egypt_, are an amazing and wonderful sight.

Modifiers that are not placed near the words or phrases that they modify are called **misplaced modifiers**.

> **Misplaced:** _Scared to death_, the black night enveloped the lost student.
> **Correct:** _Scared to death_, the lost student wandered the neighborhood.

If a modifying word, phrase, or clause does not modify a particular word, then it is called a **dangling modifier**. Every modifier must have a word that it clearly modifies.

> **Dangling modifier:** _Warmed by the sun_, it felt good to be at the beach.
> ("Warmed by the sun" does not modify "it.")
> **Correct:** _Warmed by the sun_, we relaxed on our beach towels.
> ("Warmed by the sun" modifies "we.")

GUIDE TO MISUSED WORDS

a — an
The word *a* is used before a word that begins with a consonant sound.
> Danny painted *a* picture of his friends.

The word *an* is used before a word that begins with a vowel sound.
> Patty put *an* apple in her lunch sack.
> There is still *an* hour before lunch.

accept — except
The word *accept* is a verb that means to receive or to agree to.
> I *accept* your apology,

The word *except* is a preposition that means other than.
> You can take everything *except* the bike.

affect — effect
The word *affect* is a verb that means to influence.
> His inspirational words *affected* her deeply.

The word *effect* is a noun that refers to something brought on by a cause.
> What *effect* will the rain have on the baseball game?

already — all ready
Use the time word *already* to say that you have completed a task earlier.
> I *already* finished my homework.

Use the two words *all ready* to say that you are completely prepared.
> I am *all ready* to start my homework.

and — to
And is a conjunction that means also.
> Billy *and* I are going to the park.

To is used before a present-tense verb to form an infinitive. Don't use *and* instead of *to* in an infinitive.
> **Incorrect:** Come *and* get us at the park at 6:00.
> > Try *and* get a video we'll all like.
> **Correct:** Come *to* get us at the park at 6:00.
> > Try *to* get a video we'll all like.

between — among
Use the word *between* when speaking of two persons or things.
> Ryan must choose *between* a new soccer ball and a new baseball mitt.

Use the word *among* when speaking of more than two persons or things.
> The five groups split the history projects *among* themselves.

bring — take
The word *bring* means carry to.
> *Bring* the paper in from the porch.

The word *take* means carry away from.
> *Take* this report with you when you leave.

farther — further

The word *farther* is an adjective or adverb that means at a greater measurable distance or length. Think of the word *far*, which describes a long distance or length.

Jim can jump *farther* than Kevin can.

The word *further* is an adjective or adverb that means more distant in time or degree; additional.

How much *further* do we have to drive?

fewer — less

The word *fewer* refers to things that can be counted.

We had *fewer* plants than we thought.

The word *less* refers to things that can be measured.

The success of the show was *less* than expected.

good — well

Use the adjective *good* when describing a person or thing.

That was a *good* movie.

Use the adverb *well* when telling how something is done.

Dennis plays the trumpet *well*.

healthful — healthy

Healthful is used to describe things that promote good health.

Taking vitamins and eating *healthful* food is important.

Healthy is used to describe the state of being in good health.

I eat a balanced diet to remain *healthy*.

I — me

Use *I* in a compound subject when the speaker is part of the subject. A good test is to replace the compound with just *I*.

Correct: *Mike and I* played video games with Tony.

(Test: *I* played video games with Tony.)

Incorrect: *Mike and me* played video games with Tony.

(Test: *Me* played video games with Tony.)

Use *me* when the speaker receives the action of the verb. Again, a good test is to replace the compound with just *me*.

Correct: Mike loaned *Tony and me* his video game.

(Test: Mike loaned *me* his video game.)

in — into

Use *in* to refer to something inside a location.

The towels are on the top shelf *in* the linen closet.

Use *into* to refer to a movement from outside to inside a location.

Let's go *into* the restaurant—it's freezing out here!

Dave went *into* his bedroom to get a change of socks.

its — it's

Its is a possessive pronoun.

The dog sat next to *its* bone.

It's is a contraction of "it is."

>   *It's* the perfect day for a picnic.

let — leave

Use the word *let* when speaking about allowing or permitting something.

>   Will you *let* me ride your bike?

Use the word *leave* when speaking about going away from or to somewhere.

>   We will *leave* for our meeting in one hour.

Also use *leave* to mean to allow to remain.

>   **Correct:** *Leave* the tools by the peach tree.
>   **Incorrect:** *Let* the boys alone!

lie — lay

The word *lie* is a verb that means "to rest or recline." The forms of *lie* are *lie, lies,* (is) *lying, lay,* and (have, has, or had) *lain.*

>   Mark *will lie* on the sofa.
>   Mark *is lying* on the sofa.
>   He *lay* there for two hours.
>   He *has lain* there for two hours.

The word *lay* is a verb that means "to put or place something." The forms of *lay* are *lay, lays, laying, laid,* and (have, has, or had) *laid.*

>   Kathy, *lay* your coat on the bed.
>   Kathy *is laying* her coat on the bed.
>   She *laid* her coat on the bed.
>   Kathy *has laid* her coat on the bed.

like — as if

Like is only a preposition. *Like* should never be followed by a verb.

>   That sweater is just *like* one you already have.

Use *as if* as a subordinate conjunction to introduce a clause.

>   It looks *as if* Gary and Nancy are getting along great.

loose — lose

Use the adjective *loose* to describe something that isn't tight.

>   My tooth is *loose.*

Use the verb *lose* to mean not winning.

>   We can't *lose* this game.

may — can

The word *may* is used when asking or giving permission.

>   "*May* I borrow your math book?" asked Lisa.
>   "Yes, you *may,*" said Sandra.

The word *can* is used when talking about being able to do something.

>   "*Can* you jump rope?" asked Ben.
>   "I *can* jump rope," said Jeannie.

of — off

The word *of* is used to mean belonging to something, containing something, or about something.

May I have a cup *of* milk?

Do not use the word *of* instead of *have*. Use *have* with the words *ought, must, might,* and *could.*

>**Incorrect:** He *could* of told me.
>
>**Correct:** He *could* have told me.

The word *off* is used to mean "away from" or "not on or touching" something.

>The dress fell *off* its hanger.

Do not use the word *off* instead of *from.*

>**Incorrect:** Helen borrowed some sugar *off* her neighbor.
>
>**Correct:** Helen borrowed some sugar *from* her neighbor.

Do not use the word *off* with the word *of.*

>**Incorrect:** Get *off of* the grass.
>
>**Correct:** Get *off* the grass.

principal — principle

A *principal* is the leader of a school. The princi*pal* is your *pal.*

>Our *principal,* Dr. Taylor, used to teach science.

When something is *principle,* it is important or first.

>The *principle* conductor never led the orchestra's rehearsals.

raise — rise

The word *raise* is a verb that means to "grow something" or "move upward." The forms of *raise* are *raise*(s), (is) *raising, raised,* and have *raised.*

>Ellen *is raising* the bottom shelf.
>
>We *will raise* tomatoes this year.

The word *rise* is a verb that means to "go up" or "get up." The forms of *rise* are *rise*(s), (is) *rising, rose,* and (have) *risen.*

>I *rise* at 6 each morning.
>
>The sun *has risen.*

say — go

Always use the word *say* instead of the informal *go* when writing dialogue or describing what someone said.

>**Bad:** "And then he *goes,* 'Whatever,' and just walks off."
>
>**Better:** "And then he *said,* 'Whatever' and just walked off."

since — because

The word *since* expresses a period of time.

>We've been swimming *since* 8 this morning.

The word *because* expresses a cause or reason.

>**Correct:** We're swimming *because* we love the exercise.
>
>**Incorrect:** We're swimming *since* we love it.

sit — set

The word *sit*(s) is used when speaking of resting or staying in one place.

>"Please, *sit* in the blue chair," said Mother.
>
>"Robby usually *sits* in the yellow chair," said Tony.

The word *set*(s) is used when speaking of putting or placing an object somewhere.

Connie *set* the cups on the counter.

She usually *sets* them in the sink.

that — which

Use *that* to introduce a clause without a comma.

She took the bat *that* was signed by Cal Ripken.

Use *which* to introduce a clause following a comma.

She stared at the bat, *which* lay broken on the floor, and burst into tears.

then — than

The word *then* means "at that time."

We had dinner, and *then* we washed the dishes.

The word *than* introduces the second item in a comparison.

I like the blue van better *than* the red sports car.

there — their — they're

The word *there* is used to mean in that place, to that place, or at that place.

The ball rolled over *there*.

The word *there* is sometimes used with the words *is, are, was,* and *were*.

There are five cookies on the plate.

The word *their* is used to show ownership or possession.

The students picked up *their* books.

The word *they're* is a contraction. It means "they are."

They're coming over tomorrow.

very — so

Both *very* and *so* can be used as adverbs, but do not use *so* in place of *very* to show amount or degree.

Incorrect: Yuki is *so* cute.

Correct: Yuki is *very* cute.

whose — who's

The word *whose* is a possessive pronoun.

Whose is this cup?

The word *who's* is a contraction of "who is."

Who's the owner of this cup?

your — you're

The word *your* is a possessive pronoun.

The word *you're* is a contraction of "you are."

You're going to *your* lesson whether you like it or not!

(you are)　　　(pronoun)

PRONOUN PROBLEMS

Polite Pronouns
One should be polite and always name oneself last. Therefore, "me and ___" is never correct. If the speaker is part of the subject, he or she should say "___ and I," as in "Jacob and I are allergic to cats." If the speaker receives the action of the verb or follows a preposition, he or she should say "___ and me," as in "Please give Chelsea and me any leftover candy."

Avoiding Sexist Pronouns
Pronouns must agree in number, person, and gender with the noun they refer to. Until recently, indefinite pronouns, such as *each* and *everyone*, used a masculine singular pronoun.

>Everyone has a right to his own opinion.

However, many people today believe that there are different ways of changing language to make it more neutral and that not everyone agrees on the best way of doing so. Whenever possible, replace *he*, *him*, or *his* with *he or she*, *him or her*, or *his or hers*. Just remember that subject, verb, and pronoun must agree: don't use the plural "they" in a sentence with a singular subject.

>**Correct:** Everyone has the right to *his or her* own opinion.
>**Incorrect:** Everyone has the right to *their* own opinion.

Unnecessary Words
It may be tempting to add extra words, especially unnecessary pronouns, to sentences. To avoid making mistakes, reread each sentence and link the pronouns to their antecedents. If one antecedent has more than one pronoun, one may need to be removed. Here are some examples.

>**Incorrect:** I saw that man there fixing a tire.
>The word *there* is unnecessary because *that* already points out *the man*.
>**Correct:** I saw that man fixing a tire.

>**Incorrect:** Sam doesn't have himself a new pair of shoes for school.
>*Himself* is unnecessary because it already says that *Sam* doesn't have the shoes.
>**Correct:** Sam doesn't have a new pair of shoes for school.

>**Incorrect:** These here pants are torn.
>*Here* is unnecessary because *these* tells you which *pants*.
>**Correct:** These pants are torn.

>**Incorrect:** That girl at the movies she wouldn't sit down
>The word *she* is unnecessary because *that* tells you which *girl*.
>**Correct:** That girl at the movies wouldn't sit down.

Who vs. Whom
Although *whom* is being used less frequently in informal speech, its correct usage is still preferred in formal writing. Because *whom* sounds a little like *him*, it is easy to remember

that the difference between *who* and *whom* is the same as the difference between *he* and *him*. *Who* and *he* are subject pronouns. *Whom* and *him* are object pronouns.

Who is your best friend? *He* is my best friend.
Whom did you invite to your party? I invited *him*.

Direct and Indirect Objects

A **direct object** is a noun or pronoun that answers the question, "what?" or "whom?" after the verb.

Andy watched the *parade*.
What did Andy watch? He watched the parade.
Parade is the direct object in this sentence.

Jeff took *Kelly* to the library.
Jeff took whom to the library? He took Kelly to the library.
Kelly is the direct object in this sentence.

An **indirect object** is a word that tells "to whom" or "for whom" something is done. An indirect object usually comes between the verb and the direct object.

Mother made *Sarah* a new dress.
First, what did mother make? She made a new dress. *Dress* is the direct object.
For whom did Mother make a new dress? She made it for Sarah.
Sarah is the indirect object in this sentence.

SECTION 3
MECHANICS

Mechanics are the rules for capitalization and punctuation. All the rules you need to know to write a perfectly punctuated paper are right here. In this section, you'll find rules for using commas, periods, quotation marks, and many other punctuation marks, as well as rules for using italics and underlines. You'll also find suggestions for formatting your paper. "Formatting" explains how to punctuate paragraphs, how to make a title page, and where to put your name, the date, the page numbers, and other important information on a paper.

CAPITALIZATION

Rules for Capitalization

Use a capital letter at the beginning of a sentence.

We went to the space center today.

The first word in a greeting and the first word in a closing should be capitalized.

Dear Mr. Jackson,
Sincerely, Tamara

A proper noun names a particular person, place, or thing. Every proper noun begins with a capital letter.

Jacob
Center **M**iddle **S**chool
Jupiter
Teen **M**agazine

The names of relatives, such as Father and Mother, should be capitalized when they are used as a name or with another name.

Is **M**other home yet?
Did **U**ncle **J**im call?

The first letter of titles and abbreviations of titles, such as Doctor and Mrs., should be capitalized.

Doctor Sanchez
Mr. Sanchez

Use a capital letter for initials that stand for someone's name.

J.F. Kennedy
F.D. Roosevelt

Every city name begins with a capital letter.

Jacksonville
San **D**iego

Every state name begins with a capital letter.

Florida

Michigan

The days of the week and the months of the year each start with a capital letter.

Friday

January

The names of holidays begin with capital letters.

President's **D**ay

Memorial **D**ay

The first word, last word, and each important word in a book title begin with capital letters. Do not capitalize words like *a, an, and, at, by, for, in, of,* and *the* unless they are the first word of the title.

Huckleberry **F**inn

Trumpet of the **S**wans

The word *I* is always capitalized.

Dave and **I** are going to the movies this afternoon.

When referring to the planet, *Earth* is capitalized. When referring to dirt, it is not capitalized.

I enjoy studying about our planet, **E**arth, and its moon.

The earth was dry and hard, so we used shovels and hoes to loosen the soil.

PUNCTUATION

Comma (,)

Use a comma after introductory words or phrases.

>Chris, I found your missing necklace.
>If we hurry, we can get to the bus stop in time.

Use a comma in a compound sentence—two complete thoughts joined by *and, but, or, yet,* or *for.*

>The rain poured outside the tent, but we were snug and dry in our sleeping bags.

Use a comma to separate three or more words in a series.

>Gold, silver, and copper are used to make jewelry.

Use a comma to separate three or more phrases in a series.

>Did you vacation at the beach, in the mountains, or on the ranch?

Use a comma to tell the reader to pause, or to separate the name of the person being spoken to from what is being said.

>Brandon, are you coming with us?
>Yes, my mom said I could go.

Use a comma in a date between the day of the month and the year, and after the year if the sentence continues.

>My birthday is October 30, 1992.
>On February 9, 1992, my little sister was born.

Use a comma between the city and the state, and after the state if the sentence continues.

>Kelly lives in Lexington, Kentucky.
>Kelly has lived in Lexington, Kentucky, for two years.

Use a comma after the greeting and the closing in a friendly letter.

>Dear Uncle Bob,
>I hope you are feeling much better.
>Sincerely,
>Naomi

Use a comma after the closing in a business letter.

>Yours truly,
>Samuel Foster

Semicolon (;)

Use a semicolon to combine two independent clauses in a compound sentence when a conjunction (*and, but, yet*) isn't used.

>Frank plays tennis; his sister is a swimmer.

Colon (:)

Use a colon to introduce a list or a series of things.

> For the hike, you will need the following items: sturdy shoes, thick socks, a water bottle, and a backpack.

Do not use a colon if the series follows an expression, such as *for example, namely, for instance,* or *that is.*

> We were pestered by flying insects, namely mosquitoes and black flies.

Use a colon to separate hours and minutes when writing the time.

> It is now 10:45 A.M.

Use a colon after the salutation or greeting in a business letter.

> Dear Mrs. Jennings:

Period (.)

Use a period at the end of a statement.

> I love to write.

Use a period at the end a command.

> Put the fried chicken in the picnic basket.

Use a period at the end a request.

> Please bring me that map.

Use a period after abbreviations, such as Mrs., Ave., and yd.

> Mrs. Roberts lives on Sabrina Ave.

Use a period after an initial.

> U.S. Grant was a Civil War general before he became president.

Exclamation Point (!)

Use an exclamation point at the end of a sentence that shows surprise or warning.

> Wow! You really surprised me just then.
> Watch out for falling rocks!

Question Mark (?)

Use a question mark at the end of an interrogative sentence.

> Are you going to the football game tonight?

Quotation Marks (" ")

Use quotations marks when writing exact words from a conversation. When the speaker's name comes first, use a comma before the quotations.

> Brent said, "That sounds really cool."

When the speaker's name comes last, use a comma, question mark, or exclamation point at the end of the quotation.

> "This is a special CD collection," answered Tony.
> "Why are you wearing a sling?" asked Alyshia.
> "Don't feed the bears!" warned Aaron.

When the speaker's name comes in the middle, use a comma before and after the name to separate it from the quotation.

> "Have you noticed," asked Julie, "that this playground is a mess?"

Put quotation marks around the titles of songs, poems, and stories.

> "Yellow Submarine" by the Beatles
> "Where the Sidewalk Ends" by Shel Silverstein
> "The Emperor's New Clothes" by Hans Christian Andersen

Parentheses ( )
Use parentheses to separate a list from the rest of a sentence.

> Bring your supplies (sack lunch, pencil, clipboard, worksheets) for the field trip.

Use parentheses to separate a phrase or clause from the rest of a sentence.

> Mark (who is Danny's big brother) walked into the store.

Brackets [ ]
Use brackets in a quotation to replace a word or to explain a word.

> As Alice was falling and falling down the rabbit hole, she feared that she would never stop: "I must be getting somewhere near the centre [British spelling of *center*] of the Earth," she said to herself.

Use brackets to explain something that is already in parentheses.

> *Alice's Adventures in Wonderland* has been a favorite children's story ever since its publication over a century ago (it was first published in 1865 [Macmillan], but because of printing errors, it was reprinted a year later by a second New York publisher [Appleton]).

Apostrophe (')
Use an apostrophe in a contraction to take the place of one or more letters that are taken away.

> can't, won't, shouldn't

Use an apostrophe in a possessive noun to show what belongs to whom.

> Sheila's shoes, the children's coats, the brothers' skateboards

Hyphen (-)
Use a hyphen to break a word between syllables at the end of a line in running text. The dictionary will show you where it is appropriate to break a word.

> This is our fav-
> orite place to eat.

Use a hyphen to join two-part numbers.

> twenty-one, ninety-nine

Use a hyphen to separate a prefix from a proper noun.

> pro-American

Use a hyphen to write a fraction as a word.

> one-half

Use a hyphen to join some compound nouns and adjectives.
    hurricane-like weather, our favorite baby-sitter

Dash (—)
Use a dash to separate a list from the rest of a sentence.
    Bring your supplies—sack lunch, pencil, clipboard, and worksheets—for the field trip.

Use a dash to separate a phrase, clause, or list from the rest of the sentence.
    Mark—who is Danny's big brother—walked into the store.

Ellipsis Points (...)
Use ellipsis points to mark words you left out of a direct quote.
    "The rainforest is the greatest...source of carbon dioxide on Earth."

Slashes (/)
Use slashes to mark the line breaks in a poem or play dialogue you are quoting.
    "'Tis but thy name that is my enemy;/Thou art thyself" according to Shakespeare's
    Juliet.

ITALICS AND UNDERLINES

Italics (*italics***)**
Use italics on **book titles**.
   Huckleberry Finn

Use italics on **magazines**.
   Time

Use italics on **newspapers**.
   New York Times

Use italics on **pamphlets**.
   Facts About Skincare

Use italics on **play titles**.
   Romeo and Juliet

Use italics on **film titles**.
   101 Dalmatians

Use italics on **television programs**.
   Sesame Street

Use italics on **works of visual art**.
   da Vinci's *Mona Lisa*

Use italics on **comic strips**.
   Peanuts

Use italics on **software**.
   WordPerfect

Use italics on **names of ships**, **trains**, **aircraft**, **spacecraft**.
   Titanic, Silver Streak, Spirit of St. Louis, Columbia

Use italics for **words as words**.
   We painted a large sign that said *OPEN*.

Underline (<u>Underline</u>)
Book titles are always underlined when hand written. When they are typed, they should be italicized.
   I just read <u>Holes</u> by Louis Sachar.
   I just read *Holes* by Louis Sachar.

FORMATTING PARAGRAPHS AND PAPERS

Your teacher will probably give you guidelines on how to format your paper, but here are some ideas and reminders to help you prepare a professional paper:

- Prepare a **title page** with the title, your name, and the date. Do not underline or italicize your title unless your teacher tells you to do so.
- If you don't use a title page, write the **title** at the center of the top of the first page with your name underneath it. Write the **date** in the top right-hand corner of the paper.
- Start the **first paragraph** one line below your name.
- Start **each paragraph** with an **indented sentence**.
- Your teacher should tell you if you need to **single-space** or **double-space** your paper. Keep in mind that this will affect your **page count**.
- Write the **page number** either at the bottom center of each page or in the top right hand corner. Do not write the page number on the first page. Instead, write 2 on the second page and continue from there.
- If your paper has **visual aids** or **illustrations**, clearly divide them from the text or keep them on a separate page.
- At the end of your paper, include a separate page for your **bibliography**.
- Keep all the pages of your paper together in a **folder** or use a **paper clip** or a **binder clip**. Avoid staples unless your teacher tells you to use them.

SECTION 4
WRITING

In this section you will find the five steps of the writing process, with examples on how to brainstorm, write outlines, and draw word webs. There are also tips on research: getting started, supplies you may need, and how to take notes. Later in the section you'll find definitions and examples of many types of writing, including fiction, plays, poems, expository and persuasive writing, and letters. At the end of the section is a part on assessment and rubrics, so you can judge your own writing for yourself before you publish it.

THE FIVE-STEP WRITING PROCESS

The five steps to follow in the writing process are: **PREWRITING**, **DRAFTING**, **REVISING**, **PROOFREADING**, and **PUBLISHING**.

PREWRITING—Think
- Decide on a topic to write about.
- Consider who will read or listen to your written work.
- Brainstorm ideas about the subject.
- List places where you can research information.
- Do your research.

DRAFTING—Write
- Put the information you researched into your own words.
- Write sentences and paragraphs even if they are not perfect.
- Read what you have written and judge if it says what you mean.
- Show your writing to others and ask for suggestions.

REVISING—Make it Better
- Read what you have written again.
- Think about what others have said about your writing.
- Rearrange words or sentences.
- Take out or add parts to make your writing clearer or more complete.
- Replace overused or unclear words.
- Read your writing aloud to be sure it flows smoothly.

PROOFREADING—Make it Correct
- Be sure all sentences are complete.
- Correct spelling, capitalization, and punctuation.
- Change words that are not used correctly.
- Have someone check your work.
- Recopy your work correctly and neatly.

PUBLISHING—Share the Finished Product
- Read your writing aloud to a group.
- Create a book of your work.
- Send a copy to a friend or relative.
- Put your writing on display.
- Illustrate, perform, or set your creation to music.
- Congratulate yourself on a job well done!

GETTING STARTED

These five steps of the writing process are always flowing into and influencing one another without any clear line between them. Writing does not always happen in nice, neat steps. As the writer, you might get an idea for the conclusion while writing the introduction. The more you write and use this writing process, the easier it becomes. It's like riding a bike: when you first learn to ride, you are a little unsteady and unsure of yourself, but with practice, riding becomes automatic. The writing process becomes automatic too.

PREWRITING—THINK

The **prewriting step** in the process is the biggest part of writing your paper. It may seem like a lot to do at first, but once you're done prewriting, the hardest part is over.

Deciding on the Topic
The first step of prewriting is deciding on a topic. Think about the assignment: How long is it supposed to be? What type of paper is it supposed to be?

If your teacher gives you a general subject, try to narrow down a more specific topic from that subject. Make a **word web** of different topics and connected ideas. A web is a way to brainstorm ideas by putting them into a drawing. The circle in the middle shows the main topic. The other circles contain ideas about the main topic.

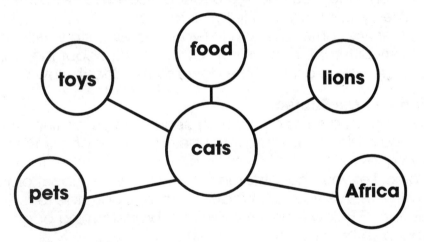

Use your word web to pick a topic that interests you. You will be spending time with this topic, and the more you like it, the more you will enjoy the research and writing you will do. You will also need to think about the **length** of your report. If your teacher wants one or two pages, you will need to have a narrower topic than if the assignment calls for five pages. You will also do a different amount of research depending on the length of the assigned report. Generally, a narrower topic will help you focus your research and make the writing of your paper easier. But be careful not to make your topic too narrow. If your topic is too specific, you may not be able to come up with enough information to write your report.

Look at the following topics. In this case, the teacher wanted the class to do a three to five page report of an aspect of the American Revolution.

The American Revolution (too broad)
Paul Revere's Light in the Old North Church (too specific)
Paul Revere (too broad)
Paul Revere's Role in the American Revolution (better)

If you have no topic, consult your **writer's journal**. Every writer should keep a notebook or journal. Write reactions to books, television, and movies. Write song lyrics you like. Write what you did that day. Write the names and brief descriptions of characters you dream up. Write settings that interest you. Write words you like and words you don't know. Just write. This journal is a great resource for your writing. Remember, the best source of ideas comes from you. When you're interested in your topic, you'll be more eager to write.

Decide on your Audience

Before you start writing or researching, decide on the audience for your paper. The audience is the group of people who will read or hear your work. If the project is a report for your class or a formal business letter, you will want to use **formal language**. However, if the project is a scary story or a friendly letter, you will probably use less formal language and your characters may use **informal language** in their dialogue. No matter what kind of writing you are doing, put your best work forward: use correct spelling and punctuation.

Also think about the purpose of your paper: will you **convince**, **inform**, or **entertain** your readers? When you convince, you change or encourage your reader's opinion in a persuasive essay. When you inform, you tell your reader all about a subject in an expository report. When you entertain, you tell your reader a story with fiction. Writing a persuasive essay is very different from writing a fable. Think about the words you will use to get your ideas across to your readers. Write down some ideas below your word web.

Brainstorm Ideas about the Subject

After you have decided on a topic and the audience of your writing, you are ready to **brainstorm**. When you brainstorm, you ask yourself questions about the topic you have chosen. Write down questions, phrases, words, or whatever comes to your mind when you think about your topic. Let your thoughts run free. Don't worry about organization, spelling, or punctuation—just write. Ask yourself: What do I know about this topic? What do I want to know about this topic? Below is an example of a brainstorming page. Use this as a model to begin your own brainstorming process.

Hurricanes

prevention?
time of year?
speed?
only over water?
where most frequent?
like a tornado?
conditions for movement over sea?
how different from typhoon?
why do they have names?

worst?
shelters?
last how long?
how to predict?
what kind of protection?
why?
what's the eye of the storm?
can I interview cousin Jackie from S.C.?

List places where you can research information

Once you've finished brainstorming, look over what you've written down and list places where you can research information on the topic. Even when you're writing a tall tale, it's a good idea to read a few tall tales yourself, just to be sure you know what is expected.

For science and history topics, use an **encyclopedia** first for an overview. Then check out an **almanac** for facts and statistics. An **atlas** may help, too. Finally, you'll want to search the **library** catalog for books and magazine articles you can use. For fiction, look up the genre, or the type of fiction, as a subject or keyword search.

There are many **resources** you can use when you write. Think about people you could interview, such as your grandparents or people in your community. Your own experience can be a great resource, too. Many authors say you should write about what you know from your own experience. This doesn't mean you can't write about aliens, dragons, or far away countries you've never been to, it just means that when you do write about those things, you should try to include ideas or problems that you have had in your own life.

Do your research

Whenever you do research, there are several steps to follow to be organized. Below is a list of supplies, ideas, and tips you can use to collect and organize your information easily.

Supplies

Use a **folder** to hold photocopies and handouts related to your report. It makes carrying all your information from school to home and from home to library easy and safe. Write your name and e-mail address or telephone number inside the folder in case you lose it.

Use **3 x 5 note cards** to write bibliography information about each source you use. Then when you write your bibliography, you can easily alphabetize the small cards. Use **4 x 6 note cards** for your notes. When you begin to write, you can lay these cards out and rearrange them as needed. This will help you organize your details before you start writing. When you research, keep a card or page in your notes set aside with the label, "dictionary words." Write down words that you don't know so you can look them up in the dictionary later. Be sure to keep **rubber bands** for each set of cards, and a **large envelope** for each set as well.

Finding Sources

Before you actually start doing your research and taking notes, you need to find sources. If your teacher would like you to use one encyclopedia, two books, two magazines, plus one additional source (almanac, atlas, biographical dictionary, etc.) you need to look at more than just one encyclopedia, more than two books, more than two magazines, etc. You want to find the information that will be the most informative on your topic. When you find a source, use your 3 x 5 note cards to keep track of the bibliography information.

- **Encyclopedia**
  Your library will likely have more than one set of encyclopedias. Use the encyclopedia's index volume and check two or three to compare the entries on your topic. It would take a long time to read all the entries, but if you read the first

and last paragraphs and the first sentence of some of the subsections of the entry, you will get a good idea of which encyclopedias will be most helpful to you.

- **Books**

When you are looking for your book sources—depending on your topic, you may find many books to choose from—check the table of contents and the index for your topic name. Again, decide which books have the most information on your topic and which will be most helpful to you when writing your report.

- **Magazines**

At the library, go to the *Reader's Guide* for magazines and copy down all the articles that have to do with your topic—there may be three or there may be ten. No matter how many, you should look up all the magazines that have information on your topic. After reading the first and last paragraphs and the first sentences of several paragraphs, decide if the article will help you. If you think you might use a particular magazine issue, write a check by the magazine information you wrote down. If you won't be using the article, cross out the information. Remember that having more than two "yes" checks is ok—you can decide which magazines will be most helpful when you do your actual note-taking later.

Skimming

Skimming is a technique you can use as you check out sources for your report. When you skim, you read quickly through the text, trying to understand the main points without slowing down for details. Skimming is an especially helpful reading technique to use when you are exploring a lengthy article or chapter for key pieces of information.

Taking Notes

After you have found your sources, you can begin taking notes. Use your brainstorming sheet. When you come to a fact or information that answers or relates to something you wrote down while brainstorming, write it down on a note card.

Note-Taking Tips

- Read the entire article or chapter before you start taking any notes—it's best to get an overview of what you are reading first to make sure you only take notes on what you need.
- Go back over the material and carefully select the information you want to include in your report. Stick with your chosen topic. Unless something seems very important, try to take notes only on information that answers the questions you wrote down during your brainstorming.
- First write the source information for your bibliography on a 3 x 5 card. Number this card (1, 2, 3). Then on a 4 x 6 card, write the question from the brainstorming sheet and the information from the source that answers that question. Write the number of the source at the top of the card.
- When you come to a fact or an idea you want to record, close the book. Think about what you've been reading, and then write the fact down in your own words. When you avoid copying right out of the book, it helps you put things in your own words and avoid plagiarizing. (See more about **Avoiding Plagiarism** in **Section 6—Research**.)

- Facts, measurements, dates, or other statistics may be copied directly. This information belongs to everyone. Just be sure to include these facts in sentences with your own words.
- If you find a whole paragraph you would like to take notes on, paraphrase and summarize the paragraph into just three sentences that condense the most important information.
- If you want to use the author's words (you may want to do this if the author is expressing an opinion), copy the words down exactly and put quotation marks around them so you won't forget that it is a quote. Then write the page number where the quote is found.

Research with Caution

When you research, be aware of the dates on your sources. You should try to use books and magazines that are not more than five years old. With some topics, such as animals, you do not need to be as careful. A book published in 1990 on the polar bear will probably have information that is just as good as a book published in 2004.

However, if you are researching any scientific, geographic, or current topic where new information is available constantly, it is best that your sources be as current as possible. In fact, magazines and the latest almanac will very likely be your best sources.

You might also find conflicting facts in the sources you use. Dates of events, especially, may be different. Do not worry about this. If you can, compare more than two sources to see if a third can help you clarify a fact.

Fact or Opinion?

In your research, you'll come across facts and opinions. It is important to know the difference so you can collect accurate information. A **fact** is a statement that is accurate. It has truth. It can be checked and supported by other facts. An **opinion** is a belief. It is someone's thought or feeling about a subject. It may or may not be true. There are certain words that may signal an opinion: *believe, feel, think, better,* or *even more.*

Scientists believe more money should be spent in studying space.
Scientists have been studying problems in space.

In the first sentence, the words *believe* and *more* are both used. This statement is the opinion of the scientists. The second statement is a fact. The scientists are studying space.

DRAFTING—WRITE

Now it is time to put the information you researched into your own words. When you have all your note cards together and all your research is done, you are ready to begin the **drafting** process. The first thing you should do is to write an outline.

Organizing an Outline

An **outline** lists the information you have gathered in the order you will write it in your paper. An outline has topics (I, II, III, IV), subtopics (A, B, C), and details (1, 2, 3).

Think of your outline as a map—this map will guide you from the beginning of your report to the end. Pretend that you are explaining your topic to a friend. What would you explain first? Second? Third? This will help you order your main ideas for the outline.

The outline, like your paper, should have a beginning, a middle, and an end. At the **beginning**, you introduce the topic and explain what you will be talking about in your report. The **middle** of the report is called the body. Here you give the reader all the details. The **end** is called the conclusion. In your conclusion, you can sum up or repeat the main idea, give your personal opinion on the topic, or give a prediction about what will happen in the future. You should only do this last type of conclusion if your topic is a current event or scientific discovery.

First, group your note cards into three sections: beginning, middle, and end. All the cards in one section should relate to the same general subtopic. Next, organize the middle part. Decide if you will use a chronological pattern (arranging the cards according to what happened in time). If your report topic is more scientific, order the cards from general facts to specific facts. If you have three or four strong subtopics, organize the cards into these groups.

Once you have your cards organized, you can write your outline. Include only the key points on the outline. Don't bother to write out the facts and details; simply list the topics or questions, so you'll know what to write next.

Outline: Life in France
- I.   Introduction to Life in France
- II.   Daily Activities
  - A. School
  - B. Entertainment
    - 1. art
    - 2. movies
- III.   Foods
  - A. Cheeses and Appetizers
    - 1. Escargot
    - 2. Foie Gras
  - B. Main dishes
  - C. Desserts

        IV.   Going to Paris
               A. Eiffel Tower
               B. Louvre Museum
               C. Arch de Triumph
        V.   Conclusion

Write sentences and paragraphs even if they are not perfect. When your outline is complete, you are ready to start writing your first draft.

Writing a Paragraph

A **paragraph** is a group of sentences that belong together. When you begin a new idea or paragraph, start on a new line and indent the first word several spaces from the left margin. A **paper** is a group of paragraphs about one topic. Sometimes a paper is so short that it is only one paragraph long. No matter how many paragraphs you write, you develop them in the same way unless you are writing a dialogue in a story. Remember, all sentences in the paragraph have a close relationship to each other.

First, develop your main idea according to a specific order. Your sentences may be written according to time, space, or order of importance. Words used to show order include: *first, last, second, next, finally, then, tomorrow, before, after, least, smallest,* or *most important.*

A paragraph starts with an introductory sentence that tells the main idea. Supporting sentences add details. Once you know your purpose and order, write smooth-flowing, supporting sentences. They give details, reasons, examples, or likenesses and/or differences. The concluding paragraph of a paper usually draws together the supporting details and restates the main idea.

Details help the reader form a clearer picture. See how these details help you picture Robin's skateboard:

    Robin enjoys her new skateboard.
    Robin enjoys her shiny, red skateboard with the turned-up, pointed front.

Reasons are provided when the writer wants to persuade the reader. Sometimes writers show how their topic is like something the reader knows. Vocabulary used to show likenesses includes *also, just as, in the same manner, resembles,* and *similarly.* To develop a paragraph that shows differences, you might include words like *by contrast, on the other hand, unlike, on the contrary,* and *but.*

Skip every other line as you write or double-space your typed paper so that there will plenty of room around the text for you to add comments, suggestions, and new sentences. Read what you have written and judge if it says what you mean. Write through your whole outline. When you've finished this first draft, read it carefully.

Staying on Topic

Staying on topic is very important to your writing. As you read your writing, ask yourself: What is the main idea of this paragraph? Do these sentences give reasons, examples, details, or facts that support the main idea of the paragraph? Remember the *W*s of writing as you read: **who**, **what**, **where**, **when**, **why**, and **how**. Do your paragraphs and sentences answer these questions? Think of your paper as a picture: each sentence is a detail and each paragraph is a group of details. Together these details make up a larger image.

Show your draft to others and ask for suggestions.

After you have read through your draft once, give it to a friend, brother, sister, or parent to read. Have him or her read only for the text—don't worry about punctuation, spelling, or other errors at this time. Have your reader ask the same questions you asked yourself: What is the main idea of this paragraph? Do these sentences give reasons, examples, details, or facts that directly relate to the main idea of the paragraph? Do the paragraphs and sentences answer the questions who, what, where, when, why, and how? Ask what your reader thinks you can do to improve the contents of your paper.

REVISING—MAKE IT BETTER

Re-Read What You Have Written
Do your math homework, play a game, take a walk, or wait until the next morning before you read your paper again. Then ask yourself the same questions. What can you do to make the contents better? Think about what others have said about your draft. Make a list of comments and suggestions your readers—and you—have thought of.

Rearrange
Start with your introduction and work through the paper, writing notes, rearranging words and sentences, and writing new sentences between the lines and in the margins. You may discover that you are missing a key fact or detail. Go back to your sources and notes if necessary to fill the gap in your research.

Replace Overused or Unclear Words
Part of improving the content of your paper is making sure every word you use means what you want it to mean. As you review your draft, use a thesaurus to look up synonyms for overused words. Replace words that confuse your readers. Read each sentence and ask yourself: what is the point I am trying to make? Condense each sentence to its main idea. Replace or remove confusing or extra words.

Read your Writing Aloud to Be Sure it Flows Smoothly
After you've made so many changes, you'll need to reread the whole paper to make sure it still flows and makes sense. This time, read it aloud. Reading aloud helps you to go slower. You'll catch more mistakes this way.

Prepare your Bibliography
At the end of a research report, you must include a bibliography to give credit to your sources. A bibliography is an alphabetical listing, by author, of the sources you used for information. Books, magazines, encyclopedias, and other sources each have their own bibliographical form.

Book:
Last Name, First Name of Author. *The Title in Italics*. Place of Publication: Publisher, date of publication.

Sail, T.H. *The Story of Boats*. Boatweave, New Jersey: Wave Press, 1989.

Magazine:
Last Name, First Name of Author. "Title of Article in Quotation Marks," Title of Magazine Underlined (Date of issue in parenthesis), pages.

Rogers, William. "How to Train your Parakeet," Pet Magazine (April 7, 1989), 85-87.

Encyclopedia:
Last Name, First Name of Author if Given. "Title of Article in Quotation Marks," Title of Encyclopedia Underlined. Year. Volume Number, pages.

"Pirates," Encyclopedia of History. 1987. Volume 18, pp. 188-191.

Internet:
Last Name, First Name of Author if Given. "Article Title in Quotation Marks," Web site address. Date revised or updated.

Needlman, Robert. "Adolescent Stress," **http://www.drspock.com/article**. June, 2003.

It is a good idea to print all Internet sources, so you will have the content and the address at the top of the page.

Bibliography Note Cards
Use the following cards as a reference to help you prepare your bibliography 3 x 5 cards during research.

Book Bibliography Card

Author: _____

Title: _____

Place of Publication: _____

Publisher: _____

Copyright Date: _____ Pages: _____

Encyclopedia Bibliography Card

Author (if given): _____

Title of Article: _____

Name of Encyclopedia: _____

Copyright Date: _____ Volume: _____

Pages: _____

Magazine Bibliography Card

Author (may come at end of article): _____

Title of Article: _____

Name of Magazine: _____

Volume Number: _____ Date: _____

Pages: _____

Internet Bibliography Card

Author: _____

Title of Article: _____

Full Web site address: http://www. _____

Date page was last revised: _____

PROOFREADING—MAKE IT CORRECT

Be Sure All Sentences Are Complete

Take another break from your paper. When you come back to it, you'll be ready to start proofreading it. Proofreading is different from revising. When you revise, you work on the quality of the content. When you proofread, you work on the correctness of spelling, punctuation, and word usage.

Start by rereading each sentence. Make sure it is a complete sentence and not a fragment. Also review your sentences to make sure they are not too long. Shorten run-on sentences by removing extra words or adding punctuation.

Correct Spelling, Capitalization, and Punctuation

Carefully read your work and correct spelling, capitalization, and punctuation errors. Does every sentence start with a capital letter? Does each sentence have the proper commas and end punctuation? Pay special attention to dialogue and sentences that use quotation marks. For help with this, use **Section 3: Mechanics**.

Check for Correct Word Usage

Homophones and words with multiple meanings can confuse you. Part of checking spelling is making sure that you used the proper spelling of words like *there, they're*, and *their*, or *scent, cent*, and *sent*. Change contractions to two words. If you used a word and you're not sure if you used it correctly, take the time to look it up in the dictionary. Make sure you used nouns as nouns and verbs as verbs—changing a word's part of speech can make it meaningless or confusing to the reader.

Proofreading Tips

Sometimes you think you wrote one thing but actually you did not. This makes it difficult for you to find mistakes in your own writing. You read what you meant to say rather than the actual words on the page. It helps to put the writing away overnight. This gives your brain time to forget what you wrote. Later, you will be able to see the words that are actually on the page. It helps to read your work aloud, word for word. Listen to see whether it makes sense. Try to identify missing or extra words. Read your work again, silently. Look carefully for mistakes in punctuation, spelling, and grammar. Find punctuation mistakes by reading the sentences aloud and backwards. Start with the last sentence, then read the next-to-last sentences, and so on. If what you read doesn't sound like a sentence, check the punctuation.

Proofread for mistakes in spelling, punctuation, capitalization, and verb usage. It is best to check your work for no more than two items at a time. Here's a proofreading checklist.

Proofreading Checklist

    I. Mechanics
        A. Spelling
            1. Use homophones correctly.
            2. Change contractions to two words.
        B. Capitalization
            1. Start all sentences with a capital letter including sentences inside dialogue.

2. Capitalize specific names of people, places, and things.

C. Punctuation
    1. Punctuate the end of each sentence properly.
    2. Place commas in compound sentences and in items listed in a series.
    3. Punctuate dialogue or conversation with quotation marks and commas.

II. Usage
    A. Check your use of commonly misused words.
    B. Check for correct subject/verb agreement.

III. Read your writing to make sure the meaning is clear and complete.

Once you've made all your changes, have a friend read it for punctuation, spelling, and word usage errors you may have missed.

Proofreading Symbols

Symbol	Meaning	Example
#	new paragraph	# Many children have lived in the White House.
≡	capital letter	Theodore roosevelt's family may have been the most spirited bunch.
/	lowercase letter	His son, Quentin, once snuck a Pony inside!
∧	insert	Why did Quentin do that He wanted to cheer up his brother.
ᶔ	delete (take out)	Theodore Roosevelt he had six children.
⊙	add a period	Archie and Quentin were the youngest ⊙
⩔	add an apostrophe	Alice was Theodore Roosevelts oldest child.
⩗	add a comma	Some people thought Alice was too wild and they criticized Roosevelt.
ᵛᵛ ᵛᵛ	add quotation marks	He responded, I can be president, or I can supervise Alice. Nobody could do both.

⌇	transpose (reverse)	The Roosevelt kids had fun in the White House.
⌐	move	They slid ⌐ on silver trays down the stairs.
• • •	stet (leave it as is)	They walked through the hallways on stilts.
#	insert space	The president even played sometimes.
◡	close up space	He liked Hide-and-Seek and pillow fights!

Write Final Copy

After you've finished revising and proofreading, you're ready to rewrite a fresh, error-free copy with all the changes you've made. Use your best penmanship or type carefully. Even if the content is a masterpiece, your readers will notice misspellings and punctuation mistakes. Put the pages in a folder or notebook for safekeeping, so they won't be folded, bent, or creased. Watch out for bad weather and the cafeteria, too. Water, mud, food, and pets are a final copy's worst enemies!

PUBLISHING—SHARE THE FINISHED PRODUCT

Now that you've got a finished product, share it! Here are some ideas for getting your writing out into the world.

Group Reading
Start an Author's Group with your friends or classmates. Get together and take turns reading your work. Then discuss each piece. Set ground rules for discussion, such as a list of questions you will ask every author, and agree to respect one another's work by taking it seriously. Don't forget to bring snacks to share!

Create a Book
Use a three-hole punch and ribbon or twist-ties to bind your pages together. You can also have your work professionally bound at a copy center. Some art supply stores have blank, pre-bound books that you can fill in for yourself. You can handwrite in your text or cut your typed pages to fit. Use illustrations, computer art and graphics, or stickers to decorate the book.

Send a Copy to a Friend or Relative
Believe it or not, your friends and relatives would love to see your creativity. You may be surprised the next time you visit to see your creation on someone's coffee table or refrigerator! Books make great gifts, too. You can write special stories for birthdays or anniversaries.

Put Your Writing on Display
Ask your librarian if you can display your work in the juvenile or young adult section of the local library. You could ask your school librarian, too. Who knows how many other people will follow your example? Putting your work on display is a great way to encourage other writers and to help writers get new ideas for their future projects.

Illustrate, Perform, or Set Your Creation to Music
If you've written a play, it's time to perform it! Remember that the most important part of putting on a play is the acting. It doesn't matter if you don't have all the props, or if you don't have a real theater in which to perform. Just do your best! The audience will appreciate your effort—and your great story!

Congratulate Yourself!
Take the time to think about your writing. What is your favorite part of the piece? What do you wish you had done differently? What was the hardest part of the process? Write down your reflections in your writer's journal. Your ideas will help you when it's time to write again!

GENRES

A **genre** is a particular type of category. In literature, there are many categories, or genres, of fiction. These include science fiction, tall tales, and mysteries, just to name a few. There are non-fiction genres, too: biography, poetry, persuasive essays, and expository reports.

FICTION WRITING

Fiction is not true. Stories, poems, plays, myths, fables, mysteries, science fiction, historical fiction, and realistic fiction are genres of fiction. Even though each type of fiction has different elements, they are all types of stories. Every story needs a problem to solve (the plot), a setting, and interesting characters. It should also have a beginning, a middle, and an end. Here are some important parts of stories.

Characters
The most important part of many stories is the **characters**. The reader has to understand and care about the characters if the story is going to be successful. The author develops characters in three ways: by what he or she shows about the character, by what the character says, and by what the character does. Good writers show; they don't tell. See the difference below between telling what a character is like and showing what a character is like.

How a character...	Telling	Showing
Looked:	He was strong.	Muscles bulged under his shirt.
Felt:	He felt sad.	A dark cloud seemed to settle over him.
Acted	She was friendly.	She smiled and waved at everyone.
Talked	She said a car was coming.	She screamed, "Watch out for the car!"

Write so your reader knows what the characters look like, say, do, think, and feel. The best way to do this is to include **sensory details** that draw upon any of the five senses—**sight, sound, smell, touch,** and even **taste**. Help the reader experience the situation just as the character did. Bring your characters to life. "Jill was sad as she watched Amy leave" is not as descriptive as "Jill sighed heavily as her best friend disappeared into the distance. Amy was headed toward a new town and a new life—without Jill."

Setting
The **setting** defines the space in which the story takes place. Think of the setting not just as the **where**, but also the **when**. Depending on the type of fiction you are writing, your story may take place in the past, present, or future. It may also take place underwater, in space, or in China. Describe the setting when it will make the most impact in the story. Use one of the first paragraphs of your story to define your space. Or tell the reader where the story takes place, but wait until later in the story to reveal your time. Deciding how and when to explain the setting can build mystery and suspense.

Plot

What happens in a story is the **plot**, or plan. The plot introduces, builds, and finally solves a problem. At the beginning of the story, the author introduces the characters and the setting. The writer also introduces a **problem**. Through the middle of the story, the characters are developed as they deal with the problem. Then, towards the end, the **climax** occurs. The climax is the answer or solution to the problem and it should be the height of the action. The end resolves any minor details and wraps up the action. The **solution** may be that there is no solution, but at least the character or characters have gained a new insight about the situation.

The plot is the heart of the story. Think of an interesting or funny problem, then think of a solution. Don't forget to explain and develop the events or episodes of the story in the proper sequence. You may tell the story chronologically from start to finish. You may decide to tell the story backwards. Be creative and decide what will work best in the story: it will help to show the reader a clear connection between the problem, the main character, and the character's feelings.

Theme

The **theme** of a story is the main point the writer wants to get across. If the story is about a struggle two friends go through, then the theme is probably the importance of friendship. If something bad happens and the main character has to get through it, then the theme could be perseverance or courage. Answer the following questions to strengthen your theme.

> What do you want your readers to think about most when they finish your story?
> Are the characters or the events in the plot more important to your message?
> What sentences, dialogue, or descriptions can you improve to make your message clearer?

Tone

The **tone** of the story is the mood that it creates. Are the characters depressed? Is the setting peaceful? The tone of the story is important to getting the theme across. Again, think about how you want your readers to feel as they read the story. If the story is about the main character's triumph, then the tone will probably be happy and light. If the main character's dog dies, then the tone will probably be depressed and sad.

The Narrator: First, Second, or Third Person

You can choose one of three plans for telling the actual story. **First person** means that the main character tells the story. He or she will talk about things from his or her point of view and use the pronoun *I* when he or she explains how he or she feels.

Second person is not very common, but it can be really creative. Second person is being spoken to. In this case, the narrator will be telling the story of what a character is doing to that character, using the pronoun *you*: "You walked out onto the sidewalk and breathed in the cool spring air. The sight of budding trees and the smell of daffodils delighted your senses."

Third person is probably the most common. Third person is being spoken about. When you write a report, you should always use the third person. You should avoid putting the word *I* in a report because you are reporting facts, not your opinion. The third person pronouns are *he, she, it,* and *they.* The narrator will tell about the characters.

You may want to try two different narrators. Let a main character tell part of the story, and then switch back to third person. Only do this if you can make an obvious break between the sections: you don't want to confuse your reader—or yourself!

Point of View

When you choose a narrator, you are also choosing the **point of view**. The point of view describes who tells the story. It is the narrator's version of the events that we will read throughout the story. This is why it works well sometimes to switch narrators. The new narrator gives the readers a new point of view on something they've already heard about from the original narrator's perspective.

Most authors do not show things from their villains' points of view. They want their readers to connect with the heroes of the story, so they show events from a hero's point of view.

Dialogue

You can record a conversation between characters using **dialogue**, but you can also develop action. Just imagine: two characters are wandering through an abandoned house in the dark without flashlights:

> "Did you hear something?" Holly breathed. She held Adam's arm tighter.
> Almost immediately Adam whispered, "What was that?"
> "There's a light...under that door," Holly replied, gesturing towards the end of the hall with her head. "What should we do?"

Here the dialogue explains what is happening without the author just telling us, adding suspense to the scene.

A **direct quotation** is the use of someone's exact words. It is always set off with quotation marks. An **indirect quotation** is the writer's description of someone else's words. It does not require quotation marks.

> direct: Brent said, "Ben is bringing the dog to the vet."
> indirect: Brent said that Ben is bringing the dog to the vet.

Foreshadowing

Foreshadowing lets the writer clue the reader in on events that will happen later in the story. The author can insert little comments with words like *if only, maybe if,* or *perhaps that's why.* These comments lead the reader to think about the possible future event. They can reduce the shock of the climax of the story. For example:

> If only Celia had listened to her mother's advice that morning.
> Perhaps that's why she didn't hear our shouts from the opposite corner.

REALISTIC FICTION

Unlike all the types of fiction above, **realistic fiction** could actually happen. It may even be based on actual events. Realistic fiction has human characters living the present that deal with everyday problems and come up with everyday solutions. The themes of realistic fiction are things we all deal with: friendships, families, loss, courage, perseverance, and growing up. Here's an example:

Emily's Play

Emily knew that this was her big chance. She stepped out onto the stage and drew in all that lay before her: the audience waiting anxiously in the half-light, her friends standing on their masking-tape marks in full costume, their shiny faces beaded with makeup. She saw her older brother close one eye ever so quickly—their special signal. She strode over to him. Slowly her lips curled up in a grin, as she said her very first line, "What a fine day for a picnic, Mr. McGillicutty."

Emily was an actress.

"Emily, you were amazing! I can't believe it!"

"Wow, what a compliment. Did you really think I would mess up my big chance?"

"Of course I did," Drew said with a twinkle in his eye. He winked.

Emily rolled her eyes. "Ha ha, Drew. You're hilarious."

Drew caught Emily in his big-brother grip and held her tight. "You were great, Em," he said seriously.

Emily pushed him away and batted at something in her eye. They grinned at each other.

Corrie, Sandra, and David rushed up to congratulate her, throwing big bouquets of daisies and carnations into Emily's arms as they kissed her cheeks and hugged her tightly. Corrie and Sandra's eyes met. They clasped hands and started dancing around in a circle, cheering, "Emily! Emily!"

Historical Fiction

Historical fiction is a lot like realistic fiction: it deals with real people and their real problems. The difference is that historical fiction is set in an historical period during an historical event. Karen Hesse's book *Out of the Dust* is a good example of historical fiction. In it, a girl tells the story of her life during the Great Depression. She explains what it was like to live during a time when people had little money because of the stock market crash. She talks about school, farm life, and her troubles, so the reader can understand what it was like to live during that period of American history.

Historical Fiction Builders

Who is the main character?
Who's telling the story?

During which historic time period does the character live?
What is the world like during this time? (Think about clothes, homes, everyday life, roles of men and women, and school.)

Which events in the plot will be from history and which will be from fiction?
What problems does the main character face?

Could this story happen today?

Mystery

Missing people, dark shadows, mysterious strangers, footsteps in the night, strange occurrences—all of these mixed together make for a good mystery story. In addition to these characteristics, there are several other factors that make a story into a mystery. The more of the following ingredients a mystery has, the better the story is likely to be:

Suspense

This is the nervous feeling you get while reading that something is going to happen, but you don't know what it is or when it will happen. Build suspense using sensory descriptions and revealing key facts slowly or unexpectedly.

Clues

A good mystery should have clues so that the reader can follow the action and try to figure out the answer before the characters figure it out in the story.

False leads

A lead is information that can be of possible use to you in a search. False leads will keep the reader wandering off the path to the real answers. False leads will keep the reader in suspense as he or she reads.

Answer these questions to write your own mystery:

Mystery Builders

Who is the detective/mystery solver?
What does (name) look like?
What is (name) like?

Who are the detective's assistants, if any?
Who are the mysterious characters (also called suspects)?

List some clues that help solve the mystery.

List any false leads in the story.

How is the mystery solved?

FANTASY

Fantasy stories could never be real. They include fantastic characters like witches, dragons, talking animals, and unicorns. Fantasies often take place in imaginary settings. Fairy tales, fables, tall tales, and science fiction are all types of fantasy writing.

Fairy Tales

We all know **fairy tales** from our childhood. Stories like *Snow White, Hansel and Gretel,* and *The Little Mermaid* are well-known fairy tales. Fairy tales are fantasy stories, because most of them have some fantastic characters or settings. Gingerbread houses, mermaids, witches, and fairies inhabit this type of fiction. Here's an example:

Cora and the Giant

Once upon a time, in a kingdom far, far away, there lived a beautiful princess named Cora. Cora never listened to what her father said, and she liked to take long walks outside the palace walls every afternoon.

One day Cora was out strolling when she heard the silver trumpets ringing their call for supper. She hadn't realized that it was getting so late, but sure enough the west was a jumble of red, orange, and pink and above her the sky was growing dark. But Cora didn't feel like going in just yet. She turned away from the castle and strode off into the darkening woods.

Almost immediately she came upon a glistening pond. Although it was growing dark, the water was crystal clear, and it seemed to sparkle like the moon in the dusk. Cora was suddenly aware of her thirst. She bent down slowly, careful not to get her dress dirty, and cupped her hands under the icy water.

With a startling whoosh of air and a cannon ball of a splash, Cora sprang back from the pond. Her startled eyes beheld a giant standing before her. He had risen eight feet out of the water and stood glowering at her, droplets dripping down from his bald green head past his deep purple eyes to his long, frowning face. Cora stared in amazement.

Fable

A fable is an old type of story. It dates back to Ancient Greece. Thinkers and writers like Socrates and Aesop used fables to get across a specific message or moral to their listeners and readers. A **fable** is a simple story with an important message, or moral, for the reader. In Aesop's fable, *The Tortoise and the Hare*, the turtle, which is much slower, wins the race because the much faster rabbit thinks he can't lose and takes unnecessary breaks. The moral of the story is that skill alone does not lead to success in life. The turtle proved that you need dedication and perseverance to succeed.

Tall Tales

Tall tales were especially popular in America when the first settlers started moving west. **Tall tales** are "tall" because they are exaggerated, incredible, and not likely to be true. They exaggerate a character's size or what he or she can do. Paul Bunyan, John Henry, Pecos Bill, and Casey Jones are popular characters from tall tales. Here's an example:

The Giant From Mars

Years ago when the world was young, a giant came down from Mars. He was fifteen miles tall and not very smart. When he lay down, he made the English Channel. He took his bath in the Indian Ocean, and he went swimming in the Atlantic Ocean. After his swim, when he put his hand on land, he made the Great Lakes. When he sat down to eat lunch, he made the Grand Canyon. Then he amused himself by making sand castles. These sand castles became the Great Smoky Mountains. After a while, he went back for another swim. This time, he made all of the valleys, and he broke a dam, which let the ice from the Arctic into the United States. This made all of our glaciers.

Science Fiction

Science fiction is a type of fantasy that uses scientific ideas and a setting controlled by scientific possibilities. Time travel, space travel, the development of new species of animals, and living in cities underwater are all science fiction topics, because they rely on scientific ideas and details. Futuristic technology is very important to science fiction.

Science Fiction Builders

Who is the main character?
Does he or she have special powers or abilities?
What is his or her goal or purpose?
How does the main character set about achieving goals or solving problems?
What obstacles does the character face?

Where and when does the story take place?

Who are the other characters?
Who's telling the story?

Describe any science-related elements of the story.
What is the climax or most exciting moment of the story?

PLAYS

A **play** is a type of fiction written just for actors who will tell the story with their words and actions on a **stage**. A play is told in **acts** and **scenes**. Plays can have one to five acts. The writer splits up the action so that it will fit into these acts. A scene takes place in one location only. Characters can come and go from that scene, but the place stays the same.

The **setting** of the play should be simple—there should only be a few different locations. The writer should describe the sets—where the scenes take place—at the beginning of the scene. A set can be as simple as a desk and chair to show that the characters are in an office. It can also have fancy background paintings that show a city skyline, or a whole set of bedroom furniture. As the writer you can make the sets as simple or as involved as you want. Remember that the characters have to explain and show everything to the audience. Include lines to help the viewer understand where the characters are: Whose house is it? Whose office is it? What building is it? What city does the story take place in?

The **characters** are the most important part of a play because they tell the whole story. The writer develops the plot using dialogue and monologue. **Dialogue** is conversation between characters. A **monologue** is a speech by one character. The audience or other characters may listen to the monologue. Monologues are a good way of giving the audience information that none of the other characters knows. It's a good way to build suspense in a mystery.

Give the character **stage directions**, too. Stage directions tell the character where to move and how to act while reading his or her dialogue. If the character has to hug her mother while saying a certain line, be sure to include that as a stage direction.

Play Builders
Title
Theme
Genre: Is the play a comedy, drama, or mystery? Is it historical, realistic, or fantastic?

Main character
Main character's personality

Another main character
This character's personality
Supporting characters

Setting (time and place)
General Plot

POEMS

A writer writes a poem to tell something or show something, just like a story. Poetry expresses the imagination with an arrangement of words and phrases. Usually, poetry is not written in complete sentences. It is just a different form of story telling. It has character, theme, tone, point of view, and description just like a story. A poem can be written in several different forms. Some are stricter than others.

Limerick
A **limerick** is supposed to be funny, silly, and ridiculous. Limericks consist of five lines. The first, second, and fifth lines rhyme with one another and have three beats. The third and fourth lines also rhyme with one another and have two beats.

> There was a young fellow named Fisher,
> Who was fishing for fish in a fissure.
> > Then a cod with a grin
> > Pulled the fisherman in. . .
> Now they're fishing the fissure for Fisher.

Concrete Poetry
Concrete poetry is written about a picture of an object, such as a ball, truck, flower, or even fingers. The object becomes part of the poem and the words of the poem are arranged around or within the object. The arrangement of the words and the object chosen should express the feeling of the poem.

Water everywhere in a large pool,
We can swim all day long if we want to.

Cinquain
A **cinquain** is based on a five-line pattern. Although there are a number of different patterns, the most often used is 1-2-3-4-1. The first line has one word, the second has two, the third has three, the fourth has four, and the fifth has one. Each line has a purpose:

Line 1 states the theme of the poem.
Line 2 describes the theme of the poem.
Line 3 provides an action for the theme.
Line 4 gives a feeling of the theme.
Line 5 states another word for the theme.

> Rain
> soft drizzle
> falls on plants
> quiet splashes of water
> Growth.

Haiku

Haiku is one of the oldest forms of Japanese poetry. Unlike cinquains, which are patterns of words, haiku is a pattern of syllables. Haiku consists of three lines of seventeen syllables total. Five syllables are in the first line, seven are in the second line, and five are in the third line. The most important thing about haiku is the feeling of the poem. Themes in haiku are usually beauty and nature.

Light dance on water
hopping from ripple to wave
Flickering light fades.

Free verse

Free verse is just that: free. A free verse poem has no set rhyme scheme, no specific number of lines, and it can be about anything you want to write about.

Indian Summer day
deep blue sky far away and laughing
Trees burn in autumn colors—see the smoke rise as wispy cloud
Miles and miles above,
Geese
in their autumn flock's "V"
swim through the sky.

NON-FICTION WRITING

Biography

A **biography** is the story of a person's life not written by that person. You may think of biographies as only being about people who lived hundreds of years ago, but biographies are written about celebrities in sports, movies, and politics every day. Check out the biography section of the library to find hundreds of biographies about all kinds of people. To write a biography, it is a good idea to use a few biographies as sources. Compare the facts and ideas in each book. Collect research for a biography just as you would for an expository report.

Biography Builders

Who is the biography about?
When did (or does) this person live?
What was (is) this person famous for?

Where and when was this person born?
What was his or her education like?
What dreams did he or she have while growing up?
What would you consider one turning point in this person's life?

Who were other people who helped this person achieve his or her goals?
Do you feel this person struggled much to reach his or her goals? Why or why not?
What affect has this person had on your life? Why did you want to write this biography?

Autobiography

An **autobiography** is the story of the writer's life. You can only write your own autobiography. *Auto* is a Greek root that means "self." Make a list of important events and people in your life. Decide on a theme and a tone for your autobiography. What do you want your readers to know about your life? Decide what message you would like to give your readers. You can write your autobiography in the first person.

Expository Reports

Expository reports give information about a subject using description, facts, or examples. Reports inform and explain. In a report that informs, the writer gives information about a topic. In a report that explains, the writer explains how to do something. Once you have chosen a topic and decided whether you need to inform or explain, make a **K-W-L chart**.

K- What I Know	W- What I Want to Know	L- What I Have Learned

First, list all the things you know about your topic in the K column. Next, list all the questions you have about your topic under the W column. Then, research the topic. List the most important things you learned about your topic in the L column. This chart is a more organized form of your brainstorming sheet. Use either a brainstorming sheet or a K-W-L chart to gather research.

Organization

The most important part of writing an expository report is organizing your information. You want your facts and details to flow in such a way that they make sense and are of interest to the reader. Here are some choices:

- ## Chronological order

Organize the facts in order of chronological time if you are writing about something that happened over time, such as a war, a famous person's life, the life cycle of an animal, or changes in climate. You will describe the events in the order they happened.

- ## Order of importance

This is a good approach if you are writing about the causes of something (such as allergies), the use of something (such as gold), or a scientist's inventions. Start with the most important item and proceed to the least important items.

- ## Problem-cause-solution

This approach is helpful for topics such as ways to avoid skin cancer, better ways to distribute the world's food, ways to save energy, or ways to solve another problem. **Describe** the problem, **explain** the cause, and **conclude** with the solution.

Here is an example of an expository report. This report explains the operation of the Pony Express to the reader. It is organized using problem-cause-solution, and by order of importance. The author introduces the problem (slow mail) and its cause (the long distance over which mail must travel) in the first few sentences. Then the author explains a solution (the Pony Express). After the introduction, the author organizes the report by order of importance.

The Pony Express

Before 1860, the mail routes from the Eastern United States to California were not very reliable. There wasn't an official mail service. Mail went on ships bound for Panama, South America. Then it was carried across tropical jungles in order to be reloaded on ships heading for the west coast. The route took about twenty-two days. Mail also went on an overland stagecoach route that took about twenty-five days. William H. Russell of the freighting firm Russell, Majors, and Waddell, believed mail should have its own service that could guarantee delivery. He developed the Pony Express and boasted that it could get mail from St. Joseph, Missouri, to Sacramento, California, faster than any other company. He hoped that the Pony Express would solve the mail delivery problem until the telegraph lines could be completed.

With the Pony Express, the mail took about ten days to cover 1,996 miles. It was carried by one of about 120 riders, who would gallop up to a relay station along the route, throw his mail pouch onto a waiting horse, and be off, all within two minutes. These relay stations were about ten miles apart and were usually located at a stream or spring. The record run over the whole line was made carrying President Abraham Lincoln's Inaugural Address in seven days and seventeen hours.

Pony Express riders were selected from the most hardy and courageous of the frontiersmen. They had to be lightweight and tough enough to ride through storms, over snowcapped mountains, across burning deserts, and through streams. They agreed not to use profane language, not to get drunk, not to gamble, not to treat animals cruelly, and not to do anything that was incompatible with the conduct of a gentleman. Each rider was given a small Bible to carry among his belongings.

PERSUASIVE ESSAY

When you write an essay, you are expressing your thoughts and opinions about a topic. In a **persuasive essay**, you encourage your readers to think the same things that you do. A persuasive essay uses argument to encourage a reader to accept the author's opinions.

First, decide what you want to talk someone into doing or believing. Narrow your topic just as you would for an expository report. Decide on an audience. Gather evidence to support your belief, or gather evidence and then formulate an opinion. Evidence includes facts and information. Learn as much as you can about your subject to make a convincing argument. Research articles, interview people, or write for information to gather evidence. Determine why you believe what you do about your subject. Remember to take notes and keep a bibliography of your sources as part of the prewriting process.

When you are ready to write your outline, you are ready to organize your arguments. The **introduction** needs to present your position with a strong statement about your stand on the issue. Organize your arguments from strongest to weakest. The strongest arguments are the ones that have the most support from your research. The weakest arguments have the least support. As you write each paragraph, start with a topic sentence that introduces the new argument. Then support that argument with facts and details. The **body** of the composition simply supports your position with clear reasons, facts, and examples as to why you believe as you do. Write a **conclusion** and include a general statement that can be drawn from the information you have collected. Your conclusion needs to be supported by the evidence you have gathered.

Persuasive Essay Builders
What is my topic?
What is my stance (how I feel about the issue)?
Who is my audience?

What are the arguments against my stance?
How can I answer those arguments?

What are the arguments for my stance?
How can I support those arguments?

What is my conclusion about the topic?

WRITING LETTERS

Business Letters

Letters are types of non-fiction, too. A **business letter** is a letter written to a company or to the government. In it, you may request information, help, express your thanks, or ask questions. The six parts to a business letter are the heading, inside address, greeting or salutation, body, closing, and signature.

- The **heading** is the address of the person who is writing the letter. Write the date under the heading.
- The **inside address** is the name and address of the company to whom the letter is being written. Each important word of the company's name begins with a capital letter.
- The **greeting** or **salutation** is the way the writer says hello. Use a colon after the greeting.
- The **body** is what is written to the company.
- The **closing** is the way the writer says good-bye. The closing always begins with a capital letter and ends with a comma. For a business letter, always say *Thank You* or *Sincerely.*
- The **signature** is the name of the person who wrote the letter.

---

207 Hope Street   _ **Heading**
Alpine, OR 97408

June 10, 2003

Sirs Import and Export, Inc.   _ **Inside Address**
64 Seventh Street
New York, NY 10022

Dear Sir: _ **Greeting/Salutation**

I have not yet received the three cartons of heirloom seeds I ordered from your company three weeks ago. I would appreciate it if this problem could be taken care of as soon as possible. _ **Body**

                    Closing _   Sincerely,

                    Allan Baynes

                    Signature _   Allan Baynes

Friendly Letters

Write a **friendly letter** as a thank-you note to someone you know well, an invitation to a party, a pen pal letter, or a letter to someone your own age.

The five parts of a friendly letter are the **heading**, **greeting**, **body**, **closing**, and **signature**. The heading of the letter can be the date or the address to which you are sending the letter. Use the greeting *Dear*, and follow it with a comma instead of a colon. In the body, write the main content of the letter. For the closing, use the word with which you feel most comfortable: *Love, Your Friend, Sincerely, Best Wishes, With Love, Many Thanks, Thank you, or Warm Regards.* Finish the letter by signing your name.

Heading _ Feb. 16, 2003

Dear Miss Judy, ___ **Greeting**

Thank you so much for being my piano teacher. I feel like I have learned so much over the past year. I really appreciate all the time you spent helping me get ready for the school talent show.

I'm sorry that we are moving and I won't get to be your student anymore. I'll miss our Tuesday practices. I promise I will keep in touch and let you know about my new teacher.

Thanks again for all your help. I will miss you! _ **Body**

Closing _ Your Friend,

Signature _ *Casey*

Envelopes

Every envelope should have the following details: **return address**, **mailing address**, and **stamp**. In a business letter, the first line of the mailing address should have the name and title of the person you want to receive the letter. The second line should have the name of the company. The third line is the street address, and the fourth line is the city, state, and zip code. For a friendly letter, you will not need to write a company name.

Barry Studios ___ **Return Address**
212 Straight A Ranch Rd.
Intelligence, AZ 85726

Mailing Address _ Mr. Michael Messa, President
Think Tank, Inc.
1026 Aikew Blvd.
Jenius, Texas 76722

WRITING ASSESSMENT

Rubrics

A **rubric** is a list of things your writing must do in order to get a certain grade. Rubrics usually have levels that are graded by numbers (1, 2, 3, 4), or words (beginning, satisfactory, capable, excellent). Each level is a little different. The teacher reads the paper and decides which category the paper fits into.

Even if your teacher doesn't use rubrics in your class, you can use these examples to help you write a better paper. If your teacher says he or she is "looking for" something in your paper, write those things down on the blank rubric. If your teacher gives you a rubric, put it in your writing folder. Then when you're in the revising stage, read your rubric and then read your paper carefully. Decide if there is anything you can do to improve your paper.

In the sample below, there are notes and tips in the parenthesis to help you understand the elements. Read each list carefully, and then decide what level your paper has achieved based on the **Scoring Levels**. Write your scoring level next to the element. Then go back to your paper and make changes to improve your score. After you've made your changes, come back to the rubric and go through it again. Do this as many times as you need to until your paper is just the way you want it.

Sample Writing Rubric
Key Elements

__ Idea Development
The paper has a main topic and facts and details that support that main topic. The introduction introduces the main idea. Each paragraph helps to develop the idea. The conclusion uses a summary to restate the main ideas.

__ Organization
Each paragraph has a topic sentence and sentences that support the topic sentence. The paper is organized in chronological (time) order (like a history essay), by three to four main points (like an animal or sports report), or from least to most specific point (like a science report).

__ Language Usage
The writer uses language correctly, including homophones and commonly misused words (check out the guide in **Section 2: Usage**). The writer uses words correctly according to their parts of speech (for example no verbs are used as adjectives). The writer also avoids double negatives, uses pronouns properly, and makes subjects and verbs agree (check out tips in **Section 5: Style**).

__ Sentence Structure
The writer uses a variety of sentence types (simple, compound, compound-complex, and complex) and a variety of sentence lengths (count your words). There are no fragments or run-ons.

__ Mechanics

The writer uses correct spelling, capitalization, and punctuation. Every paragraph is indented.

Scoring Levels

0 points—no key elements evident
1 point—beginning…few key elements evident
2 points—satisfactory…all 5 key elements evident to a moderate degree
3 points—capable…all 5 key elements evident ranging from moderate to high degree
4 points—excellent…all 5 key elements evident consistently to a high degree

Your Personal Writing Rubric
Key Elements

__ 1. _____
_____
_____

__ 2. _____
_____
_____

__ 3. _____
_____
_____

__ 4. _____
_____
_____

__ 5. _____
_____
_____

Scoring levels

0 points—no key elements evident
1 point—beginning…few key elements evident
2 points—satisfactory…all 5 key elements evident to a moderate degree
3 points—capable…all 5 key elements evident ranging from moderate to high degree
4 points—excellent…all 5 key elements evident consistently to a high degree

Checklists

A **checklist** is like a rubric because both are lists of things you should do in your paper. A checklist, however, does not have a grade that goes with it. When you go through a checklist, make notes of what you need to do to improve your paper, and give yourself credit for what you are already doing well. The checklist is here to help you check yourself and your work before you hand it in. In the samples below, you'll find lists of things to help you focus on one part of your paper. Use these ideas during the revising process to help you improve your work without worrying too much about the grading.

Organization Checklist

__ Events and Ideas in Order that Makes Sense
Use chronological (time) order for history, specific points (see the "Life in France" example under **How to Write an Outline**), or least to most specific for a science paper.

__ Main Idea in Each Paragraph
Every paragraph has a topic sentence. Reread each topic sentence. Separate it into complete subject and predicate. Then separate the simple subject and predicate. Is the sentence direct? Does it say what you want it to say?

__ Details, Descriptions, Examples Focus on Topic
Every sentence in a paragraph relates back to the main idea. It gives a fact or detail to support the main idea. Go back to your outline. Does every sentence in your paragraph relate back to something you wrote in your outline?

__ Ending Summarizes Main Ideas/Points Made
The conclusion should be a summary of the main points of the essay. Don't introduce new facts or details. Don't list every detail again. Reread your topic sentences and make a list of the main points they make. Then restate these points in the conclusion.

Usage and Style Checklist (review **Section 2: Usage** and **Section 5: Style**)

__ Language Usage
The writer uses language correctly, including homophones and commonly misused words (check out the guide in **Section 2: Usage**). The writer uses words correctly according to their parts of speech (for example no verbs are used as adjectives) and makes subjects and verbs agree.

__ Uses Formal Language
The writer avoids contractions, slang, clichés, and idioms. The writer avoids sloppy speech (gonna, coulda, hafta). The writer also avoids double negatives and uses pronouns properly.

__ Sentence Structure
The writer uses a variety of sentence types (simple, compound, compound-complex, and complex) and a variety of sentence lengths (count your words). There are no fragments or run-ons.

__ Formatting
The writer indents each paragraph. The writer uses punctuation correctly. The writer has the title, his or her name, the date, and the page numbers written or typed on the paper.

SECTION 5
STYLE

Style is important to all writers. Style describes the quality of your writing: Are the sentences clear? Are the length and type of sentences varied throughout the paragraph? Do the sentences flow together smoothly? Do all the sentences in a paragraph stay on topic? This section on style is focused on helping you write the clearest, best quality sentences and paragraphs that you can. You'll find tips for improving your sentences and paragraphs and advice on how to make them flow and work together better. Every sentence will say what you want it to say, and every paragraph will stay on topic and flow smoothly.

RULES FOR BETTER SENTENCES

Remove Extra Words
Tighten wordy sentences by removing extra words. Read each sentence. Condense it into a simple subject and a simple predicate. Then consider the complete subject and complete predicate. Does your point come across without all the extra words?

Slaves were portrayed or stereotyped as…

Take out the word *portrayed*. You don't need both *portrayed* and *stereotyped* to get your point across.

Parallel Construction
All parts of a sentence should be alike, or parallel. When writing lists, make sure that each part of the list is written in the same way. Pay special attention to gerunds and infinitives, and be careful when you write comparisons.

Wrong: The horses were sleek, streamlined, and fed proper food.
Right: The horses were sleek, streamlined, and properly fed.

Wrong: The group likes to swim, to ski, and go fishing.
Right: The group likes to swim, to ski, and to fish.

Wrong: Going to the store is not as interesting as it is to watch a movie.
Right: Going to the store is not as interesting as watching a movie.

Wrong: To drive at night is more difficult than daylight driving.
Right: Nighttime driving is more difficult than daylight driving.

Subjects That Follow Verbs
When subjects follow verbs, make sure that the subject and verb agree in number.

At the back of the room are several empty chairs.

Several empty chairs is the subject of the sentence, so the verb, *are*, must agree with this plural subject. *At the back of the room* is a prepositional phrase, not the subject.

Add Needed Words
When you make sentences parallel, don't forget to add any words you may need around conjunctions.

Incorrect: Some clubs believe and live by the old rules.
You can't "believe by" something.
Correct: Some clubs believe in and live by the old rules.
You "believe in" and "live by."

Give More Detail

Nouns are sometimes used within a sentence in an **appositive**, a word or phrase set off by commas that identifies or gives further details about another noun. The examples below show how an appositive expands a sentence.

OK: Abraham Lincoln gave his most famous speech at a dedication ceremony for a Civil War cemetery.
Better: Abraham Lincoln gave his most famous speech, the Gettysburg Address, at a dedication ceremony for a Civil War cemetery.
OK: Ms. Walker was out of breath from racing Craig.
Better: Ms. Walker was out of breath from racing Craig, the fastest boy in our class.

Avoid Shifts in Verb Tense

When you start a sentence in the present tense, try to stay in the present tense.

Incorrect: She patted the puppy's head to wake it. Finally it *opens* its eyes.
Correct: She patted the puppy's head to wake it. Finally it *opened* its eyes.

Avoid Misplaced Words

Reread your sentences and make sure all adverbs are placed as close as possible to the words they modify.

Incorrect: You will *only* need to plant *one* packet of seeds.
Correct: You will need to plant *only one* packet of seeds.

Misplaced and Dangling Modifiers

The complete subject or complete predicate of a sentence usually contains words or phrases called **modifiers**. Modifiers add to the meaning of a sentence.

The ancient tombs, *which stand powerfully on the hot sands of Egypt*, are an amazing and wonderful sight.

Modifiers that are not placed near the words or phrases that they modify are called **misplaced modifiers**.

Misplaced: *Scared to death*, the black night enveloped the lost student.
Correct: *Scared to death*, the lost student wandered the neighborhood.

If a modifying word, phrase, or clause does not modify a particular word, it is called a **dangling modifier**. Every modifier must have a word that it clearly modifies.

Warmed by the sun, it felt good to be at the beach.
(dangling modifier—"warmed by the sun" does not modify "it")
Warmed by the sun, we relaxed on our beach towels.
(correct—"warmed by the sun" modifies "we")

Plural and Singular Antecedents

When replacing a noun with a pronoun, be sure the noun and pronoun agree in number. With some collective nouns, such as *team, class,* and *group,* you need to use a singular pronoun.

Correct: I asked how I could get on the soccer team, and *the team members* told me to try out for a position.

Incorrect: I asked how I could get on the soccer team, and *they* told me to try out.

Confusing Ownership

Frequently we come across sentences that can be understood in two or more ways.

Bad: Paul went with Dad to get his hat.

Whose hat is it? Paul's or Dad's? Instead of the pronoun "his," the writer should use the noun again.

Better: Paul went with Dad to get Dad's hat.

Formal Writing, Formal Language

In a formal paper like a report, business letter, or essay, it is better to use formal English. This means you should avoid using contractions, slang, clichés, idioms, and one-word sentences or interjections. Here are some examples from a business letter to help you.

Contractions

Bad: This wasn't what I expected when I ordered your product.

Better: This was not what I expected when I ordered your product.

Slang

Bad: This product really stinks and I want my money back.

Better: This product did not do what it was supposed to do, and I would like a refund.

Clichés and Idioms

Bad: Don't get hung up on excuses, just send me my money.

Better: I would appreciate an immediate refund.

Interjections

Bad: Really! I can't believe your company is still in business.

Better: Thank you for your attention to this matter.

Sloppy Speech

Sloppy speech is another thing you should avoid in formal writing. When we speak with our friends or family, we often use sloppy speech—slurring two words into one. This is okay for speech, but be sure to use the full words in your formal writing. The only time you might want to use these slurred words is when writing dialogue to develop the speaker's character.

Common Sloppy Speech

woulda	would have
gotta	got to
wanna	want to

Avoid Double Negatives

Two negatives equal a positive. Therefore, if you want a sentence to have a negative meaning, use only one negative word.

12 SPELLING RULES

English spelling is crazy for the most part. However, there are a several patterns you can rely on to help you spell words correctly. On the following pages, you'll find a dozen spelling rules that are helpful. One hint in reading the rules: Take your time. Read each rule and example carefully and then stop to think about it. Try to relate the rules to the examples. Think of your own examples, too.

C-Enders

When *c* is the last letter of a word, it is always hard. That means it is pronounced like a *k*. When adding *ing, er,* or *y* to such words, first insert a *k*:

>   panic—panicky
>   picnic—picnicking
>   traffic—trafficking

The *k* is said to "protect" the hard sound of the *c*. Without the *k*, the *c* might appear to have a soft sound (*s*) as it does in a word like *icing*.

Note that you don't add the *k* when the suffix begins with a consonant. When adding *ing* to *mimic*, for example, it becomes *mimicking*. But when the suffix *ry* is added, *mimic* becomes *mimicry* (the *k* is not needed to protect the *c* in this case).

Compound Words

When spelling a compound word—a word formed from two other words—keep both words whole. Do not drop the last letter of the first word. Do not drop the first letter of the last word. Simply push the two words together.

>   side + walk = sidewalk

This rule is true even when the resulting compound words have a strange-looking double letter in the middle.

>   book + keeper = bookkeeper
>   hitch + hiker = hitchhiker
>   room + mate = roommate

The classic exception to this rule is *pastime*.

>   past + time = pastime

Contractions

Since many contractions have homonyms, mix-ups are common. Be sure you have the right word. The trick is to expand the contraction to be certain that you have the right word. Suppose you wrote:

>   I gave the dog it's bone.

Try expanding *it's*. You get:

>   I gave the dog it is bone.

The *it is* obviously makes no sense here. Thus, the correct word is *its*.

Remember to put the apostrophe in the right place. The apostrophe goes in the spot where the letters were removed. Again, expanding the contraction is a good test. Suppose you wrote *are'nt*. Check it by expansion: *are'nt = are not*. The *o* in *not* is dropped in making this contraction. That means the apostrophe should go between the *n* and the *t*. Hence, the correct spelling is *aren't*.

Double-Enders

When the last two letters of a single-syllable word are a vowel followed by a consonant, double the consonant before adding a suffix.

> rip—ripper, ripping
> swim—swimmer, swimming
> top—topping, topped

The same rule holds for multiple-syllable words when the final syllable is accented.

> acquit—acquittal
> control—controlling
> submit—submitting

Note that words like *seat* become *seating* (one *t*) because there are two vowels before the final consonant. Words like *help* become *helping* (one *p*) because they end in two consonants. And words like *benefit* become *benefited* (one *t*) because they are not accented on the final syllable.

E-Enders

Many words end in a silent *e*. Two rules govern what happens to this *e* when you add suffixes.

First rule: Drop the *e* when the suffix begins with a vowel—*ed, ing, ous, able, y.*

> lose—losing
> louse—lousy
> nerve—nervous
> prove—provable
> tease—teasing

Important exceptions to this rule are *noticeable* and *courageous*. Also, with many words that end in *ve*, it is permissible to either drop or keep the *e* before *able*.

> love—lovable, loveable
> move—movable, moveable

Second rule: Keep the silent *e* when the suffix begins with a consonant—*ment, ful, ly.*

> care—careful
> move—movement

Judgment and *acknowledgment* (no *e*) were once exceptions to this rule, but now *judgement* and *acknowledgement* (with the *e*) are accepted. Two more exceptions— *truly* and *ninth*—drop the expected *e*'s.

Ful-Enders

Here's a truth that's short and sweet and very *powerful*. Words that end in *ful* and mean "full of" always end with *ful* (one *l*): *helpful, insightful, sorrowful*. There are no exceptions. Isn't that *wonderful*?

I Before E

The most famous spelling rule of all is a jingle that goes like this: *I before e except after c or when sounded as a as in neighbor or weigh.*

| **i before e** | thief | yield |
| lie | field | |

| **except after c** | receive | receipt |
| conceive | deceive | |

| **sounded as a** | rein | heinous |
| reindeer | inveigh | |

There is a problem with this classic truth. There are at least ten exceptions that "disprove" this rule. To remember them, think of this silly phrase: *Neither leisured foreign counterfeiter could seize either weird height without forfeiting protein.*

Ly-Enders

When the suffix *ly* is added to a word, that root word usually stays the same. Hence:
> clear—clearly
> sincere—sincerely
> slow—slowly
> undoubted—undoubtedly

Two well-known exceptions are *truly* (from *true*) and *wholly* (from *whole*).

This partial *ly* truth is especially helpful when facing words that end in *lly*.
> conceptual—conceptually
> hopeful—hopefully

When you're not sure if a word ends in *lly*, try to find the root. For example, *practically* comes from *practical*. The *ly* is simply tacked on to the end.

Nay-Sayers

Nearly a dozen prefixes turn root words into their opposites.
able—unable
possible—impossible
adjusted—maladjusted
sense—nonsense

The root never changes when a negative prefix is added. In *misshape* and *unnatural*, the double letters up front may look strange, but the rule holds firm. All you have to know for sure is how the root word begins.

Suppose, for example, you have written *unecessary* (one *n*). Is that correct? You know the word means "not necessary." *Necessary* is the root. To turn it into its antonym, you must add the prefix *un*. Hence *unnecessary* (two *n*'s) is the right spelling. The same goes for *illegal*, *misspell*, and *immature*.

Occasionally, you'll have a bit of trouble figuring out the root. *Innocent*, for example, is based on *in-nocent* (*nocent* being Latin for "harmed"). Usually, though, the roots will be obvious, and you'll know to add the prefix.

il**legible**
ir**religious**

The Nay-Sayers' truth should also help you with words like *imagination* (one *m*). This is not a negative form because *agination* is not a word.

Ness-Enders
When adding the suffix *ness* to a root word, simply add the suffix. The root does not change unless it ends in *y* (happy—happiness).

close—closeness
helpful—helpfulness

Remembering that the root does not change will help you with tough words like:

mean—meanness
sudden—suddenness

O-Enders
Rules about plurals seems to multiply. Luckily, plurals don't cause many problems. Nouns that end in *o*, however, are tricky. The following observations may help.

If a vowel comes before the final *o*, add *s*:

radio—radios
rodeo—rodeos

If a consonant comes before the final *o*, add *es*:

hero—heroes
potato—potatoes

However, the plural forms of *mosquito* and *tornado* can go either way—*s* or *es*.

There is one general exception. The plural of most music-related, *o*-ending words are formed by adding *s* only.

piano—pianos
solo—solos

Y-Enders
When a word ends in *y*, change the *y* to *i* before adding the suffixes *ly, ness,* or *age*. You can slay some of the worst demons using this rule.

busy—business
day—daily
easy—easily
empty—emptiness
lonely—loneliness
penny—penniless
marry—marriage
satisfactory—satisfactorily
temporary—temporarily

There are only a few exceptions.

shy—shyly
sly—slyly

Remember to keep the *y* when adding *ing* even though it may look a little odd.

HOW TO STUDY SPELLING WORDS

1. Look at the word.
2. Copy the word.
3. Say the word aloud.
4. Spell the word aloud.
5. Write the word.
6. Check the spelling.

You can also copy the following chart to help you study.

Copy the word.	Say it aloud. ✓	Spell it aloud. ✓	Close eyes. Spell it. ✓	Fold the paper. Write the word.
1.				1.
2.				2.
3.				3.
4.				4.
5.				5.
6.				6.
7.				7.
8.				8.
9.				9.
10.				10.
11.				11.
12.				12.
13.				13.
14.				14.
15.				15.
16.				16.
17.				17.
18.				18.
19.				19.
20.				20.

100 LIFELONG WORDS

Remember how to spell these frequently used and often misspelled words.

about	grade	something
address	guess	store
again		suppose
a lot	haven't	surprise
although	having	
always	hear	taught
around	heard	teacher
	here	their
because	hour	there
been	house	they're
before		thought
birthday	knew	threw
bought	know	through
busy		to
	language	together
calendar		tomorrow
children	many	tonight
come		too
coming	name	two
could	new	
couldn't	none	until
		used
didn't	often	
different	once	very
does	only	
doesn't	our	way
done		wear
	people	weight
early	picture	we're
easy	pretty	were
enough	probably	when
every		where
everybody	receive	which
	remember	while
favorite	right	women
first		would
friend	said	write
	school	
girl	should	your
goes	some	you're

MORE FREQUENTLY MISSPELLED WORDS

accept
absence
advice
all right
arctic
beginning
believe
bicycle
broccoli
bureau
ceiling
cemetery
changeable
conscious
decease
deceive
definite
descent
device
disastrous
embarrass
exercise
fascinate
February
fiery

fluorescent
foreign
government
grateful
guarantee
harass
height
humorous
independent
jealous
jewelry
judgment
ketchup
knowledge
leisure
library
license
maintenance
mathematics
miniature
miscellaneous
misspell
mysterious
necessary
neighbor

nuclear
occasion
occurrence
piece
pigeon
playwright
prejudice
privilege
probably
pumpkin
raspberry
rhythm
science
scissors
separate
sincerely
special
thorough
truly
Tuesday
until
Wednesday
weird

NATIONAL SPELLING BEE

The Louisville, Kentucky, *Courier-Journal* started the National Spelling Bee in 1925. They hoped that the cash prizes and the trip to the capital city would encourage spellers across the country to get involved.

In 1941, The Scripps Howard News Service took over the bee. There have been as few as 9 and as many as 250 contestants over the years. In 2002, Pratyush Buddiga, the 13-year-old champion, won $12,000 cash and other prizes for spelling *prospicience* correctly. Listed below are the winning words and some of their definitions.

2002 prospicience: the act of looking forward; foresight
2001 succedaneum: a person or thing that takes the place or function of another
2000 demarche: a course of action or maneuver
1999 logorrhea: excessive talkativeness or wordiness
1998 chiaroscurist: an artist who specializes in *chiaroscurro*
1997 euonym: a name well suited to the person, place, or thing named
1996 vivisepulture: the act or practice of burying alive
1995 xanthosis: yellow discoloration of the skin from abnormal causes
1994 antediluvian: made or developed a long time ago
1993 kamikaze: a member of the Japanese air attack corps assigned to make a suicida crash on a target
1992 lyceum: a hall for public lectures or discussions
1991 antipyretic: an agent that reduces fevers

1990 fibranne	1970 croissant	1950 haruspex	1930 fracas
1989 spoliator	1969 interlocutory	1949 dulcimer	1929 asceticism
1988 elegiacal	1968 abalone	1948 psychiatry	1928 albumen
1987 staphylococci	1967 chihuahua	1947 chlorophyll	1927 luxuriance
1986 odontalgia	1966 ratoon	1946 semaphore	1926 abrogate
1985 milieu	1965 eczema	1943-45 No Bee	1925 gladiolus
1984 luge	1964 sycophant	was held.	
1983 Purim	1963 equipage	1942 sacrilegious	
1982 psoriasis	1962 equamulose	1941 initials	
1981 sarcophagus	1961 smaragdine		
		1940 therapy	
1980 elucubrate	1960 troche	1939 canonical	
1979 maculature	1959 cacolet	1938 sanitarium	
1978 deification	1958 syllepsis	1937 promiscuous	
1977 cambist	1957 schappe	1936 intersning	
1976 narcolepsy	1956 condominium	1935 intelligible	
1975 incisor	1955 custaceology	1934 deteriorating	
1974 hydrophyte	1954 transept	1933 propitiatory	
1973 vouchsafe	1953 soubrette	1932 knack	
1972 macerate	1952 vignette	1931 foulard	
1971 shalloon	1951 insouciant		

SECTION 8
VOCABULARY

This vocabulary section is designed to help you read and write better. In the reader's vocabulary, you'll find tips on homonyms, root and base words, prefixes, and suffixes. Knowing about these types of words will help you build your vocabulary. The writer's vocabulary has information on figurative language and many ideas that you can use to improve your fiction writing.

Just remember that to correctly use vocabulary, you must understand the parts of speech and how they are used. For example, the word *excruciating* is an excellent adjective to describe great pain. "My toothache was *excruciating*." However, if you use the word as a verb, "My toothache *excruciating* me," or as a noun, "The *excruciating* made me cry," your sentence will be incorrect. When in doubt about how to use a word, look it up in the dictionary or review **Section I on Grammar**.

READER'S VOCABULARY

Homonyms
Homonyms are words that sound the same but have different meanings and spellings. Homonyms can cause writers big problems. Read the following sentences.

> One mourning while weighting four the school bus, I felt a pane in my heal. It seams I had a whole inn my shoe and a peace of glass was cot inside.

See all the mistakes? The writer didn't pay attention to the spelling and meaning of those misused homonyms. The following sentences are correct.

> One morning while waiting for the school bus, I felt a pain in my heel. It seems I had a hole in my shoe and a piece of glass was caught inside.

Here is a list of commonly misused homonyms.

their/there/they're	aunt/ant	stationary/stationery	pail/pale
too/to/two	plane/plain	kernel/colonel	hi/high
your/you're	fare/fair	straight/strait	serial/cereal
its/it's	hall/haul	sight/site/cite	cell/sell
who's/whose	write/right/rite	piece/peace	weak/week
know/no	pear/pair/pare	would/wood	maid/made
feat/feet	rows/rose	steel/steal	main/mane
dew/do/due	toe/tow	grown/groan	lone/loan
week/weak	rowed/road/rode	meet/meat	hear/heard
ate/eight	sow/so/sew	through/threw	break/brake
flower/flour	knew/new	by/bye/buy	great/grate
scent/cent/sent	in/inn	heel/heal	bear/bare
weather/whether	see/sea	deer/dear	cheep/cheap
	sun/son	principal/principle	pair/pare/pear
	blew/blue	where/wear/ware	whole/hole

Homographs

The word *homograph* has two roots: *homo*, which means "the same," and *graph*, which means "write." **Homographs** are words that are written the same, having the same spelling. Homographs are even pronounced the same way sometimes, but they have different meanings. That's because each meaning comes from a different root. Take the word *hatch* for example. *Hatch* can be used to describe a chick coming out of its egg, markings someone has carved on a wall, or a door leading to a ship's cargo area.

hatch—bring forth young

hatch—to draw, cut, or engrave fine lines

hatch—an opening in a ship's deck

Watch out for homographs in your writing. Look them up in a dictionary to be sure you have used these tricky words correctly.

Context Clues

Often you can guess what a word means from the clues given by other words in the sentence. For example, you may never have heard the word *illegible*. But if your teacher says, "I cannot read this paper because your handwriting is illegible," you could guess without the help of a dictionary that *illegible* means "impossible to read." Discovering the meaning of a word by looking at the other words in a sentence is called learning from context. This skill plays an important role in developing a good vocabulary.

Context clues can also help you write a report that any reader will be able to clearly understand. When you use new vocabulary that you have learned while researching your report, be sure to use context clues to define any new concept words you used. For example:

Many submarines of the Civil War did not have *periscopes*, which allow the drivers to look above the water while the submarine is submerged. As a result, the drivers had to rely on other instruments to figure out where they were going.

Your readers may not know exactly what a *periscope* is, but by using context clues in the sentence, you can help them figure out that it is something used to look above the water.

Concept Words

A **concept word** is a word that has to do with a certain topic or idea. When you write about baseball, you may use the words *base, home run,* and *strike*. These are all baseball concept words. When you write about playing music, you may use the words *key, sharp,* and *time signature*. These are music concept words.

When you write a report about a topic that's new to you, be sure to learn the concept words that will help you explain your topic clearly. When you are researching your topic, look up words you don't know in the dictionary. You can also use the glossary of a book to help you find definitions.

Synonyms and Connotation

Synonyms are words that mean the same thing. *Big* and *large* are synonyms. Sometimes words that are synonyms have different shades of meaning. For example, *slim, skinny, slender,* and *scrawny* are synonyms. But while slim and slender are positive adjectives, *skinny* and *scrawny* give a negative sense of being too thin or ugly. A word's shade of meaning is called its *connotation*.

Connotation can also be defined as the "feeling" meaning rather than the literal dictionary definition that you get from a word. *Denotation* is the exact dictionary meaning of a word. Pay attention to the connotation, or feeling, of words that you use. When describing a dark and stormy night, you would not use the adjective *fluffy* to describe the clouds. *Fluffy* has a positive connotation. Instead, you could describe the clouds as *jagged, racing,* or *monstrous*. These words have the dark connotation you want.

You can use synonyms to improve your writing. A thesaurus is an excellent source of synonyms. While describing a perfect day, if you find yourself using *beautiful* too many times, a thesaurus will remind you of words like *dazzling* and *sparkling*—words that are more exact and descriptive. When using a thesaurus, beware of choosing a word whose exact meaning you do not understand. For example, *remark* and *yell* are both synonyms for *say*, but they have very different meanings.

Antonyms
Antonyms are words that have opposite meanings. *Tiny* and *huge* are antonyms. Use antonyms in your writing to help you stress an important point. When two things you are describing are very different, use antonyms to describe them. You can find antonyms at the end of thesaurus entries. To find words meaning *unhappy*, you could look up *happy* and find several antonyms such as *sad, melancholy,* or *miserable*.

Sensory Words
Sensory words are words that describe the senses. They explain and describe what a character sees, tastes, hears, smells, or touches. Sensory words are mostly adjectives, adverbs, and verbs. Add sensory words throughout your writing to make scenes more exciting and feelings stronger. Some words are used so often or can have so many different meanings that they do not give exact descriptions. These words usually can be replaced with synonyms that are more exact. When you see overused words in your writing, use a thesaurus to help you replace them with sensory words that are stronger and clearer.

Overused Words

nice	bad	happy	pretty
cute	said	sad	went
good	scary	great	came

Vivid Verbs

absorb	glare	rattle	smack
bolt	inspect	rip	swoop
decline	laud	sandbag	zoom
ebb	peek	scream	
glance	praise	screech	

Adjectives

beaming	deceitful	intriguing	quizzical
beefy	enchanting	inviting	sinister
bulky	engrossing	lustrous	vast
curious	glossy	magnificent	wicked
dark	immense	moldy	

Onomatopoeia

Onomatopoeia is a word that sounds like the sound it describes. Onomatopoeia words are excellent sensory words that add color and interest to your writing. Here is a list of useful onomatopoeia words.

ruff	bark	cluck	clop
clip	drip	murmur	rustle
chirp	clack	oink	howl
neigh	clang	crash	honk
cluck	clatter	snap	hiss
cock-a-doodle-doo	bong	swish	sizzle
moo	blink	smack	burp
baa	zip	smash	buzz
sigh	zoom	squeak	crack
giggle	meow	squeal	
drop	purr	roar	

Prefixes

A **prefix** is one or more syllables added to the beginning of a word to change the word's meaning. Many words have prefixes. By learning the meaning of the most common prefixes, you will be able to add many new words to your vocabulary. Here is list of common prefixes and their meanings.

Prefix	Meaning	Example
pre	before	prefix, preview
post	after	postpone, postgame
de	from	decide, debate
re	again	recreate, recharge
col	with	collect, collage
com	with	combine, comfort
con	with	concert, connect
mis	wrong	misbehave, misspell
un	not	unclear, untrue
im	not	improper, impossible
in	not, into	inactive, infects
mid	middle	midway, midnight
sub	beneath	submarine, subway
under	below	underneath, underline
semi	half, partly	semicircle, semifinal
super	more than	supernatural, superpower

auto	self	automobile, autobiography
un	not	unhappy, unpleasant
uni	one	unicycle, unicorn
bi	two	bicycle, bilingual
tri	three	tricycle, triangle
quadr	four	quarter, quadrant
pent	five	pentagon
quint	five	quintet
cent	hundred	century, cent

Suffixes

A **suffix** is a syllable, group of syllables, or a word added to the end of a word to change its meaning or part of speech. Here is a list of common suffixes and their meanings.

Suffix	Definition	Example
ist	person who does, makes, or practices	scientist, dentist
less	without or lacking	homeless, jobless
ness	state of quality of being	kindness, likeness
ly	when, how, like, or in the manner of	quietly, calmly
fy	to make or cause to be or become	beautify, purify
ize	to cause to be or become	hypnotize, realize
ion	state or quality of	nation, hibernation
ry	state or quality of	bravery, forgery
ry	place	bakery, grocery
ment	thing	ornament, instrument
ism	state or quality of	heroism, sexism
logy	study or science of	biology, zoology

Root and Base Words

Many words consist of one or more Greek or Latin roots. For example, the Greek root *tele* means "far." When it is combined with *vis*, the Latin root for "see," we get *television*—an invention that lets us *see* pictures coming from *far* away.

Here is a list of Greek and Latin roots. Use this list as a reference to help you use words correctly in your writing.

Greek Number Prefixes

Number	Prefix	Number	Prefix	Number	Prefix
one	mon	six	hexa	eleven	hendeca
two	di, bi	seven	hepta	twelve	dodeca
three	tri	eight	octa	hundred	hecta
four	tetra	nine	ennea		
five	penta	ten	deca		

Greek Prefixes

A-, AN-: without, not:
agnostic, anarchy

ACRO-: a point, topmost, at the tip:
acrobat, acrophobia

ANA-: back, again, according to:
anabolism, anachronism

ANTI-: against:
antibacterial, antidote

APO-: off, away from:
Apocrypha, apostle

AUTO-: self:
autobiography, autocracy

CAT-, CATA-: down, against, mind, remember:
cataclysm, catacomb

DIA-: through, across, over:
diabolic, diagonal

DYS-: ill, bad:
dyslexia, dystopia

ECTO-: without, on the outside:
ectoderm, ectopic (pregnancy)

EN-: in:
encapsulate, endemic

ENDO-: within, internal:
endocrine, endometrium

EPI-: upon, over, at, near:
epicenter, epidermis

ESO-: inward:
esoteric, esotery

EU-: good, well:
eulogy, euphoria

EXO-: outside, external:
exoskeleton, exothermic

HYPER-: over:
hyperactive, hyperbole

HYPO-: under:
hypocritical, hypodermic

MACRO-: large:
macrocosm, macroglobulin

META-: among, between, changed:
metabolic, metaphysics

MICRO-: small:
microphone, microwave

MISO-, MISA-: hate:
misogyny, misanthrope

PALIN-: back, again:
palindrome, palingenesis

PAN-: all:
panacea, pandemic

PARA-: beside, beyond:
parabolic, parallel

PERI-: around:
perimeter, periphery

POLY-: many:
polygamy, polygon

PSEUD-: false:
pseudepigrapha, pseudonym

SYM-, SYN-: together:
sympathy, synonym

TELE-: at a distance:
telegram, telephone

XENO-: foreign, strange:
xenon, xenophobia

Greek Roots

ANGEL: messenger:
angel, archangel, evangelist

ARCH: to rule, begin:
archangel, monarch, anarchy

ARCH: ancient, old:
archaeology, archaic, archetype

ASTRO, ASTER: star:
astronaut, asterisk, disaster

ATHL: a prize, contest:
athlete, decathlon

ATMO: vapor, gas:
atmometer, atmosphere

BIBLI: book, papyrus, scroll:
bibliography, biblist
(bible)

BIO: life:
biological, autobiography

BLEM, BOL, PARL: to throw:
problem, symbol, diabolic,
parliament

CHROM: color:
chromatic, chromolithography

CHRON: time:
chronology, anachronism

COSM: earth, world:
cosmic, cosmopolitan

CYCL: cycle, wheel:
cyclone, bicycle, recyclable

DEM, DEMO, PLEB: the people:
demagogue, endemic, democracy,
plebeian

DERM: skin:
dermatosis, epidermis

DEUTERO: second:
Deuteronomy, deuteropathy

DICHO: in two parts:
dichogamous, dichotomy

DIPLO: double:
diploid, diplopod

DOX: to praise, worship:
doxology, orthodox
(dogma)

DROME: to run:
dromedary, palindrome

DYNA: force, power, strength:
dynamic, dynasty

ECO: ecology:
ecosystem, ecotype

ELECTRO: electric:
electrolyte, electromagnetic

ERG, URG: work:
energy, surgeon

ETHNO: race, nation:
ethnocentrism, ethnography

GAM, GAMY: marriage:
bigamist, polygamy

GEO: earth:
geographic, geology

GNOS: to know:
Gnosticism, agnostic, diagnosis
(physiognomy)

GRAM, GRAPH: write:
gramophone, telegram, graphic,
autograph, autobiography

HELIO: sun:
heliocentric, heliotrope
(helium)

HETERO: different:
heterogeneous, heterologous

HOMO, HOMEO: same:
homosapien, homeopathic

HYDR: water:
hydrate, hydraulic

IDO: form, shape:
idol, kaleidoscope
(idyll)

LEXI, LOG, LOGUE: word, to speak:
lexicographer, dyslexia, catalog,
dialogue

LITH: stone:
lithography, Paleolithic

LOG, LOGY: word, study of:
logic, biological,
chronology

MAT, METRO: mother:
matrimony, metropolitan

METRO: measure:
metrology, metronome

NAU: ship:
nausea, astronaut

NECRO: corpse:
necrophilia, necropsy

OD: way, journey:
period, episode

ONYM: a name:
acronym, patronymic
(onomatopoeia)

OSTEO: bone:
osteopath, osteoporosis

PALEO: ancient, old:
Paleolithic, paleontology

PATH: to suffer:
pathology, sociopath,
homeopathic

PATRO: father:
patronize, patronymic

PED: child:
pediatrics, orthopedic

PHIL: love:
philosopher, necrophilia

PHOB: fear:
phobia, acrophobia

PHON: sound:
phonics, microphone

PHOTO: light:
photocopy, photography

PHYS: nature:
physics, physiology

POD: foot:
podiatry, tripod

POLI: city:
police, politics, cosmopolitan,
metropolis

PSYCH: mind:
psychology, psychosis

PYR: fire:
pyre, pyromaniac

SCHIZO: split:
schizoid, schizophrenia

SCOPE: see, look at:
horoscope, microscope
(bishop)
(episcopal)

SOPH: wisdom:
sophisticate, philosopher

THE: a god:
theology, atheism, pantheon

THERM: heat:
thermoelectric, thermostat

THES: to put, place:
thesis, antithesis
(apothecary)

TOM, TOMY: to cut:
atom, appendectomy

TOP: a place:
topic, utopia

TRI: three:
triangle, tripod

ZOO: animal:
zoo, zoology

Greek Suffixes

–AST: one associated with:
enthusiast, gymnast

–IA: pathological condition, territory,
pertaining to:
malaria, Romania

–ICS: thing having to do with:
ethics, politics

–ISM: action, condition, doctrine:
barbarism, criticism

–IST: makes, advocates:
apologist, socialist

–ITE: native, adherent, a part of
a body, rock/mineral:
Israelite, sulfite

–OID: resembling:
factoid, humanoid

Latin Numbers

Number	Prefix	Number	Prefix	Number	Prefix
zero	nihil	five	quinque	ten	decem
one	una	six	sex	hundred	centum
two	duo	seven	septem	thousand	mille
three	tres	eight	octo		
four	quattuor	nine	novem		

Latin Prefixes

AB–: from, by:
abdicate, abduct

AMBI–: around, about:
ambidextrous, ambiguous

ANTE–: before:
antebellum, antecedent

BENE–, BENI–: good, well:
benediction, benign

CIRCUM–: around:
circumcise, circumference

CO–, COM–: together:
coalition, communist

CONTRA–: against, facing:
contraband, contradict

DE–: down, away, off, utterly:
debase, descendant

DIS–: otherwise, apart:
disable, disconnect

EX–: out, off, away, thoroughly:
example, expatriate

EXTRA–: outside:
extracurricular, extradite

IN–, IM–, EN–: in, into, on:
inquest, important, enchant

IN–, IL–, IM–, IR–: not:
infinite, illogical, impartial, irreverent

INFRA–: below, beneath, inferior to:
infrasonic, infrastructure

INTER–: between:
interact, intermural

INTRA–: within:
intramural, intravenous

JUXTA–: near, beside:
juxtapose, juxtaposit

MAGNI–: great, large:
magnificent, magnify

MULTI–: many:
multicultural, multifaceted

NE–, NON–: not:
negate, nonchalant

OB–: toward, across, opposite:
object, obverse

PER–: through, by means of:
percent, perennial

POST–: after:
postdate, postpartum

PRE–: before:
prejudice, president

PRO–: in favor of, forward, instead of, before:
prodemocracy, prologue

RE–: again, back:
reactor, realign

RETRO–: backward:
retroactive, retrograde
(retreat)

SE–: aside, apart:
seclude, secret

SEMI–: half:
semiannual, semicolon

SUB–: beneath, secretly:
subterfuge, subterranean

SUPER–: above:
superfluous, superior

TRANS–: across, over:
transcend, transfer

Latin Roots

ACT, GATE, GEN, GI, GU: to act, do, drive:
actual, enact, reactor, fumigate, agenda, agitate, ambiguous

AERO: air, gas:
aerodynamics, aerosol

AL: to feed, nourish, grow:
alimentary, coalition
(adolescence)
(adulthood)

AMA, AMO: to love:
amateur, amorous, enamored

ANIM: mind, soul:
animate, equanimity

ANNI, ANNU, ENNI: year:
anniversary, annual, semiannual, perennial

BAT: to beat:
battery, acrobat, debate

CAD, CAS, CID: to fall:
cadaver, decadence, casualty, occasion, accident, coincide

CAL, CHA: to be warm, hot:
calorie, scalding, nonchalant

CANT, CHANT: to sing:
cantata, descant, incantation, chant, enchant
(accent)
(incentive)

CAP, CAPT, CAS, CHAS, CEIT, CEIV, CEPT, CIP, CUP: to seize, lay hold of, contain:
capable, captive, case, chase,

conceit, deceive, accept, anticipate, occupy

CENTRI: center:
centrifuge, centripetal (force)

CIT, CIV: citizen:
city, civil

CLOS, CLUDE, CLUS: to shut, close:
closet, conclude, exclusive
(claustrophobia)
(cloister)

COGN, GNOR, NOTI: to get to know:
cognitive, recognize, ignore, notice
(acquaintance)

CRED: to believe, trust:
credible, accredited
(creed)
(grant)
(miscreant)

DAT, DIT: to give:
data, edit, tradition
(traitor)
(rendezvous)
(vendor)

DEXT: on the right, skillful:
dexterity, ambidextrous

DIC: to tell, to say:
dictator, benediction, contradict, judicial
(judge)

DISCI: to learn:
disciple, discipline

DOC: to teach:
doctor, document

DON: to give:
donate, pardon, condone

DOU, DUB, DUO, DUP: two:
doubt, indubitably, duo, duplicate
(dual)
(duet)

EAS, JAC, JECT, JET: to lie, throw:
easy, adjacent, reject, trajectory, jettisoned

EGO: I:
egocentric, egotistic

ERR: to wander:
erratic, aberrant

EV: age:
longevity, medieval

FAC, FACE, FACT, FEAS, FEAT, FECT, FEIT, FIT, FIC, FICE: to make, do:
faculty, surface, fact, feasible, feature, refectory, forfeit, profit, artificial, sacrifice

FER: to bear, bring, carry:
fertile, transfer, circumference

FLU: to flow:
fluorescent, influenza

FORM: form, shape:
formula, conform, reformatory

GEN: race, kind:
gender, general

GRAC, GRAT, GREE: beloved, dear, pleasing:
grace, gratuity, agree

GRAD, GRESS: to go, step, walk:
grade, biodegradable, congress, aggression

IT: to go:
itinerate, circuit, ambitious
(ambience)
(errant)
(perishable)

JUR, JUS: to swear:
jury, perjure, justice

LAT: carried, borne:
latitude, legislator

LEG: law:
legislator, privilege

LEV: to lighten, lift, raise:
lever, elevate

LITER: letter of the alphabet:
literature, alliterate

LONG: long:
longevity, prolong, elongated

MAN: hand:
manipulate, manual

MAN: to remain:
mansion, permanent
(remain)

MED: middle:
median, medieval
(mean)
(middle)

MISE, MISS, MIT, MITT: to send:
compromise, mission, dismiss, admit, permitted

NOM: name:
nomenclature, denomination

OMNI: all:
omnipotent, omnivore

PAR, EQU: equal, peer:
par, comparison, equanimity

PAR: to give birth to, come in sight:
parent, postpartum

PATRI: father:
patriarch, patriot
(paternoster)

PED: foot:
pedigree, biped, centipede
(impeach)

PEL, PUL: to drive:
pelt, propel, pulse, compulsive

PEN, PEND, PENS, POND: to weigh, hang, pay:
pensive, pendant, depend, pension, dispense, ponder

PORT: to carry:
report, transport, important

PUN, PUNC: to point, stab:
pun, punctuate, compunction
(poignant)
(point)

QUEST, QUIR, QUIS: to seek:
quest, inquest, inquire, prerequisite

QUI: quiet, rest:
quit, requiem

ROG: to ask:
rogue, derogatory, interrogate

SAL, SULT/XULT: to leap, spring forward:
salmon, result, exultation

SCEN, SCEND: to climb, leap:
descendant, ascend, condescend
(scan)

SCI: to know:
science, conscious, omniscient

SCRI: to write:
scripture, describe, postscript

SECU/XECU, SEQU, SUIT: to follow:
consecutive, execute, sequel, pursuit
(sect)
(segue)
(intrinsic)

SED, SESS, SID: to sit, settle:
sediment, session, possess, president, reside
(hostage)

SEMBL, SIMIL, SIMUL: like, at the same time:
assemble, similar, simulate

SEN: old, old man:
senate, senile

SEN, SENT: to be, exist:
absence, present

SIGN: a mark, seal, sign:
signature, assign, designate

SOL: alone:
solo, desolate

SOL: sun:
solar, insolate

SON, SOUND: to sound:
sonar, resound

TEMP: time:
temporary, extemporaneous

TERR, TERRA: earth, land:
territory, terrarium, mediterranean

ULT: last, beyond, extremely:
ultimate, penultimate
(outrageous)

USE, UTI: to use:
use, abuse, utilize

VIT, VIV: to live:
vitamin, vivid, survive
(viable)

VOC, VOK: to call, voice:
vocation, advocate, invoke

VOR: to devour:
voracious, carnivorous

Latin Suffixes

–ACIOUS: tending to:
audacious, bodacious

–CLE, –CULUM: means, instrument, place:
particle, curriculum

–ILE: relating to, capable of:
docile, fragile

–ION: the act or result of, state or process:
hydration, oxidation

–IUM: the act, something connected with the act:
equilibrium, solarium

–MENT: result or means of an act:
adornment, advancement

–OR: act or condition of, one who performs an action:
accelerator, squalor

Imported Words

Imported words are English words that come from other languages, such as French, Arabic, or Japanese. Like Latin and Greek roots, many imported words have been used in the English language for a very long time. Many dictionaries give an etymology, or short word history, to tell what language a word comes from originally. Here is a list of commonly used imported words.

catalogue	toboggan	July	museum
carrousel	Texas	August	hypnosis
boulevard	Michigan	September	panic
question	pecan	October	jovial
bouquet	Alabama	November	titanic
budget	hickory	December	comrade
crayon	Alaska	Sunday	caravan
menu	raccoon	Monday	bungalow
lieu	moccasin	Tuesday	scant
bandage	January	Wednesday	solo
rare	February	Thursday	clan
cinema	March	Friday	asphalt
tepee	April	Saturday	
opossum	May	cereal	
Canada	June	geology	

Compound Words

Compound words are words made up of two or more base words. They can be written as one word, two words, or with a hyphen to connect them. Compound words can take the place of a long explanation and make a statement clearer.

Ben was happy to meet his *mom's new husband's son* for the first time.
Ben was happy to meet his *stepbrother* for the first time.

WRITER'S VOCABULARY

Literal v. Figurative Speech

When people say something that you know is untrue but is being said to make a point, you say they are using a **figure of speech**. Authors use figurative language to make their writing more interesting.

I was so hungry I could have eaten an elephant.

When people say something true, they are speaking **literally**. They are saying exactly what they mean.

I was so hungry I ate a bowl of hot soup and a cheese sandwich.

Idioms

An **idiom** is a phrase that has a non-literal, or figurative, meaning. Non-literal means that the words in the phrase, when understood by their dictionary meanings, do not literally mean what the phrase says. For example, *caught a cold* is an idiom. The speaker did not literally run around with a net until he or she caught the cold. The speaker means he or she got a cold.

It is fine to use idioms in your informal or fiction writing. But avoid idioms in your formal, non-fiction writing. People who speak English as their second language do not know idioms as well as native speakers, and idioms can be hard to learn. In formal writing, you want everyone who picks up your paper to be able to read it. Your reader may have trouble if you've used a lot of idioms. Here is a list of common idioms to avoid.

pull a fast one
do the honors
for the birds
cost an arm and a leg
caught a cold
ahead of time
drop me a line
in the same boat
take the rap
lose your temper

get away with it
get the picture
get up on the wrong side
    of the bed
really opened my eyes
the writing's on the wall
make ends meet
give your right arm
see eye to eye
on the ball

burn up
blow out
get lost
pull through
hang out
keep your head up
go back on your word
turn the tables

Clichés

A **cliché** is an overused phrase or idea, such as "early to bed, early to rise makes a man healthy, wealthy, and wise." Avoid clichés at all cost. These phrases are old and tired and because they've been around so long, they make your writing unclear. Replace clichés with words that say what you really mean. Here is a list of clichés to avoid.

If you can't beat them, join them.
Actions speak louder than words.
Absence makes the heart grow fonder.
Don't count your chickens before they've hatched.
The early bird catches the worm.

Waste not, want not.
Beggars can't be choosers.
Look before you leap.
You can't have your cake and eat it too.
Like father, like son.
A rolling stone gathers no moss.
A picture is worth a thousand words.
Every cloud has a silver lining.

Imagery
Once you understand the idea behind figurative language, you will be able to understand **imagery** as well. *Imagery* comes from the root word *image*, which means *picture*—something you can see. When you write using the device of imagery, you write so vividly and creatively that readers can see what you are writing in their imaginations.

Simile and Metaphor
Metaphors and **similes** are comparisons that are made for color or emphasis. Similes use *like* or *as* to compare two unrelated things. Metaphors do not use *like* or *as* but make a direct comparison.

>**simile:** The cat looked like a carved statue.
>**metaphor:** The fog was a gray blanket that lay over the town.

Symbolism
A **symbol** is a literal thing, place, or happening in writing that has a figurative meaning.
>Leaving the bright daylight of the May afternoon, he entered the gloomy darkness of the piano teacher's parlor. Another week had passed, and Bob still hadn't been practicing.

In the first sentence, *light* can symbolize peace of mind, while the *darkness* and *gloom* can symbolize the uncertainty and anxiousness Bob feels because he hasn't prepared for his lesson. Writers use symbolism to add depth to their writing. Instead of telling you that Bob feels anxious or uncertain, the writer shows you by using symbolism.

Personification
Personification is exactly what it sounds like—giving an inanimate object, like a rock or a chair, human qualities.
>Dressed in its best, glowing from head to toe, and standing perfectly straight and tall, the old house seemed brand new as it welcomed Susan in from the cold.

Sound Devices
Because there are fewer words in a poem than in a story, every word in poetry is important. By writing or arranging words in a certain way, the author makes words and phrases sound a certain way to set the tone of the poem.

Onomatopoeia is a term for words that sound like the sound they describe. Buzz, pop, snap, and fizz are all words displaying onomatopoeia.

Alliteration is a sound device, too. Starting every word in a phrase with the same letter is

alliteration. Using a soft sound like *s* makes a poem feel gentle. Using harsher tones like *k* or *r* make a poem sound tougher.

> Shining sun shone down on Susan as she sowed her sapling seed.

Assonance is like alliteration. Every word in a phrase starts with a similar vowel sound.

> The always awful authors often arrive on time.

Comparison and Contrast

To set two objects or ideas apart, compare or contrast them. To compare, list reasons why the two things are the same. Choose the strongest connection and circle it. To contrast, list reasons why the two things are different. Choose the strongest contrast and circle it. Then use these comparisons and contrasts in your writing.

An **oxymoron** is a figure of speech in which contrasting terms are put next to each other.

> There was a *deafening silence*.
> The party was a *sad celebration*.
> Jake was a *cold* person with a *warm* heart.

Comparison and contrast can be especially helpful in developing characters. When two characters are very different, show that difference with a point of contrast. When they are very similar, use a comparison to draw your reader's attention to this fact.

Rhyme Schemes

The word *scheme* means *pattern*, so a **rhyme scheme** is a pattern of rhyme used in a poem. How to use rhyme is up to the poet. For that reason, there are many different types of rhyme schemes.

When two lines that appear back to back rhyme, they are called a **couplet**.

> The light of sunset on the bay
> Always takes my cares away.

When there are four lines, and the first line rhymes with the third and the second rhymes with the fourth, it is an **a-b-a-b** pattern rhyme.

> One day in May
> While by the sea
> I ran away
> When you looked at me

Poetry can also be written in **free verse**. Free verse is poetry that doesn't rhyme or follow a specific rhyme scheme. The author writes freely.

> This is a free verse
> So it doesn't have to rhyme
> I can say what I want
> Without worrying about it.

APPENDIX 1: THE NEWBERY MEDAL

The Newbery Medals honor achievement in children's writing. Each year, a winner is announced. Here is a complete list of Newbery winners. To find out more about the award, visit the American Library Association's website at http://www.ala.org/alsc/newbery.html.

2003: *Crispin: The Cross of Lead* by Avi (Hyperion Press)
2002: *A Single Shard* by Linda Sue Park (Clarion Books/Houghton Mifflin)
2001: *A Year Down Yonder* by Richard Peck (Dial)
2000: *Bud, Not Buddy* by Christopher Paul Curtis (Delacorte)
1999: *Holes* by Louis Sachar (Frances Foster)
1998: *Out of the Dust* by Karen Hesse (Scholastic)
1997: *The View from Saturday* by E.L. Konigsburg (Jean Karl/Atheneum)
1996: *The Midwife's Apprentice* by Karen Cushman (Clarion)
1995: *Walk Two Moons* by Sharon Creech (HarperCollins)
1994: *The Giver* by Lois Lowry (Houghton)
1993: *Missing May* by Cynthia Rylant (Jackson/Orchard)
1992: *Shiloh* by Phyllis Reynolds Naylor (Atheneum)
1991: *Maniac Magee* by Jerry Spinelli (Little, Brown)
1990: *Number the Stars* by Lois Lowry (Houghton)
1989: *Joyful Noise: Poems for Two Voices* by Paul Fleischman (Harper)
1988: *Lincoln: A Photobiography* by Russell Freedman (Clarion)
1987: *The Whipping Boy* by Sid Fleischman (Greenwillow)
1986: *Sarah, Plain and Tall* by Patricia MacLachlan (Harper)
1985: *The Hero and the Crown* by Robin McKinley (Greenwillow)
1984: *Dear Mr. Henshaw* by Beverly Cleary (Morrow)
1983: *Dicey's Song* by Cynthia Voigt (Atheneum)
1982: *A Visit to William Blake's Inn: Poems for Innocent and Experienced Travelers* by Nancy Willard (Harcourt)
1981: *Jacob Have I Loved* by Katherine Paterson (Crowell)
1980: *A Gathering of Days: A New England Girl's Journal, 1830-1832* by Joan W. Blos (Scribner)
1979: *The Westing Game* by Ellen Raskin (Dutton)
1978: *Bridge to Terabithia* by Katherine Paterson (Crowell)
1977: *Roll of Thunder, Hear My Cry* by Mildred D. Taylor (Dial)
1976: *The Grey King* by Susan Cooper (McElderry/Atheneum)
1975: *M. C. Higgins, the Great* by Virginia Hamilton (Macmillan)
1974: *The Slave Dancer* by Paula Fox (Bradbury)
1973: *Julie of the Wolves* by Jean Craighead George (Harper)
1972: *Mrs. Frisby and the Rats of NIMH* by Robert C. O'Brien (Atheneum)
1971: *Summer of the Swans* by Betsy Byars (Viking)
1970: *Sounder* by William H. Armstrong (Harper)
1969: *The High King* by Lloyd Alexander (Holt)
1968: *From the Mixed-Up Files of Mrs. Basil E. Frankweiler* by E. L. Konigsburg (Atheneum)

1967: *Up a Road Slowly* by Irene Hunt (Follett)

1966: *I, Juan de Pareja* by Elizabeth Borton de Trevino (Farrar)

1965: *Shadow of a Bull* by Maia Wojciechowska (Atheneum)

1964: *It's Like This, Cat* by Emily Neville (Harper)

1963: *A Wrinkle in Time* by Madeleine L'Engle (Farrar)

1962: *The Bronze Bow* by Elizabeth George Speare (Houghton)

1961: *Island of the Blue Dolphins* by Scott O'Dell (Houghton)

1960: *Onion John* by Joseph Krumgold (Crowell)

1959: *The Witch of Blackbird Pond* by Elizabeth George Speare (Houghton)

1958: *Rifles for Watie* by Harold Keith (Crowell)

1957: *Miracles on Maple Hill* by Virginia Sorenson (Harcourt)

1956: *Carry On, Mr. Bowditch* by Jean Lee Latham (Houghton)

1955: *The Wheel on the School* by Meindert DeJong (Harper)

1954: *...And Now Miguel* by Joseph Krumgold (Crowell)

1953: *Secret of the Andes* by Ann Nolan Clark (Viking)

1952: *Ginger Pye* by Eleanor Estes (Harcourt)

1951: *Amos Fortune, Free Man* by Elizabeth Yates (Dutton)

1950: *The Door in the Wall* by Marguerite de Angeli (Doubleday)

1949: *King of the Wind* by Marguerite Henry (Rand McNally)

1948: *The Twenty-One Balloons* by William Pène du Bois (Viking)

1947: *Miss Hickory* by Carolyn Sherwin Bailey (Viking)

1946: *Strawberry Girl* by Lois Lenski (Lippincott)

1945: *Rabbit Hill* by Robert Lawson (Viking)

1944: *Johnny Tremain* by Esther Forbes (Houghton)

1943: *Adam of the Road* by Elizabeth Janet Gray (Viking)

1942: *The Matchlock Gun* by Walter Edmonds (Dodd)

1941: *Call It Courage* by Armstrong Sperry (Macmillan)

1940: *Daniel Boone* by James Daugherty (Viking)

1939: *Thimble Summer* by Elizabeth Enright (Rinehart)

1938: *The White Stag* by Kate Seredy (Viking)

1937: *Roller Skates* by Ruth Sawyer (Viking)

1936: *Caddie Woodlawn* by Carol Ryrie Brink (Macmillan)

1935: *Dobry* by Monica Shannon (Viking)

1934: *Invincible Louisa: The Story of the Author of Little Women* by Cornelia Meigs (Little, Brown)

1933: *Young Fu of the Upper Yangtze* by Elizabeth Lewis (Winston)

1932: *Waterless Mountain* by Laura Adams Armer (Longmans)

1931: *The Cat Who Went to Heaven* by Elizabeth Coatsworth (Macmillan)

1930: *Hitty, Her First Hundred Years* by Rachel Field (Macmillan)

1929: *The Trumpeter of Krakow* by Eric P. Kelly (Macmillan)

1928: *Gay Neck, the Story of a Pigeon* by Dhan Gopal Mukerji (Dutton)

1927: *Smoky, the Cowhorse* by Will James (Scribner)

1926: *Shen of the Sea* by Arthur Bowie Chrisman (Dutton)

1925: *Tales from Silver Lands* by Charles Finger (Doubleday)

1924: *The Dark Frigate* by Charles Hawes (Little, Brown)

1923: *The Voyages of Doctor Dolittle* by Hugh Lofting (Lippincott)

1922: *The Story of Mankind* by Hendrik Willem van Loon (Liveright)

APPENDIX 2: PROOFREADER'S MARKS

Proofreader's marks can be used to correct sentences and paragraphs. Here are the most frequently used marks.

Symbol	Meaning	Example
#	new paragraph	Many children have lived in the White House.
≡	capital letter	Theodore roosevelt's family may have been the most spirited bunch.
/	lowercase letter	His son, Quentin, once snuck a Pony inside!
∧	insert	Why did Quentin do that He wanted to cheer up his brother
ℛ	delete (take out)	Theodore Roosevelt ha had six children.
⊙	add a period	Archie and Quentin were the youngest
⌄	add an apostrophe	Alice was Theodore Roosevelts oldest child.
⋀	add a comma	Some people thought Alice was too wild and they criticized Roosevelt.
⌄ ⌄	add quotation marks	He responded, I can be president, or I can supervise Alice. Nobody could do both.
∼	transpose (reverse)	The Rooosvelt kids had fun in the White House.
[	move	They slid on silver trays down the stairs.
• • •	stet (leave it as is)	They walked through the hallways on stilts.
#	insert space	The president evenplayed sometimes.
⌒	close up space	He liked Hide-and- Seek and pillow fights!

EDITOR: MARTIN WINDROW

OSPREY
MILITARY

MEN-AT-ARMS SERIES · 137

THE SCYTHIANS
700-300 BC

Text by
Dr E V CERNENKO
Colour plates by
ANGUS McBRIDE
from reconstructions by
Dr M V GORELIK

First published in Great Britain in 1983 by
Osprey, an imprint of Reed Consumer Books Ltd.
Michelin House, 81 Fulham Road,
London SW3 6RB
and Auckland, Melbourne, Singapore and Toronto

British Library Cataloguing in Publication Data

Cernenko, E. V.
    The Scythians, 700–300 B.C.—(Men-at-Arms
    series; 137)
    1. Scythians
I. Title   II. Gorelik, M. V.   III. Series
    939.55 curr DK34.S4 C4 1996

    ISBN 0–85045–478–6

Filmset in Great Britain
Printed through World Print Ltd, Hong Kong

Editor's note

Authors, illustrator and editor are pleased to record
their gratitude to Dr. Heinrich Härke for his
invaluable help, without which this book could not
have been published, and to Dr. Michael Vickers for
his prompt assistance.

Introduction

The text which follows is a translation from the Russian original commissioned by Osprey from the distinguished Soviet archaeologist Dr. E. V. Cernenko, of the Archaeological Institute of the Academy of Sciences of the Ukrainian SSR. The acting head of that institute's Scythian Department, Dr. Cernenko has been active in the excavation of Scythian tombs for many years. The colour plates by Angus McBride are based upon reconstructions prepared for this book by Dr. M. V. Gorelik of the Oriental Institute of the Academy of Sciences of the SSSR, Moscow. Much of the written and pictorial material in this book is published here for the first time in the West.

Although little known to non-specialists in this period and region, the Scythians were a dominant influence in south-East Europe and the Middle East for more than three centuries, being roughly contemporaneous with the Classical Greek world. They were the first of the great armies of horse-archers out of the East which were to have such an impact upon the consciousness of Europe at intervals over about 1,000 years. Yet they were not, like the Huns and Mongols, a Turco-Mongoloid race, but straight-featured Indo-Europeans: we know this from surviving pictorial metal-work, and from the few scraps of their language which come down to us through the Greek historians.

Their mastery of the horse and the bow raised them from obscurity of nomadic stock-raisers of the steppes to the status of a major military power. At different periods they clashed—hard, and bruisingly—against the Assyrians, the Medes, the Persians, and the Macedonians. In the centuries of their greatness they ruled a huge area of what is now the Soviet Union; interestingly, they seem to have retained their nomadic ways, while establishing an apparently stable relationship with the vassal communities of settled farmers from whom they took tribute in a systematic way.

Although they left no written record, we know more of the habits and appearance of the Scythians than we do of many more recent cultures. The southern part of their range met the northern limits of the Greek world in the Greek trading cities along the north shores of the Black Sea; and it was here that

Herodotus, 'father of history', gathered the impressions of them which are still today our major written source. Here, also, they encountered skilled Greek metalsmiths. It is our good fortune that these violent, colourful, hard-drinking barbarians had a great love of decorative work in precious metals; a great wealth of such metals; the good taste to commission Greek master-craftsmen; and funerary customs which have preserved these precious relics for the study of the historian.

The Editor

The Scythians lived in the Early Iron Age, and inhabited the northern areas of the Black Sea (Pontic) steppes. Though the 'Scythian period' in the history of Eastern Europe lasted little more than 400 years, from the 7th to the 3rd centuries BC, the impression these horsemen made upon the history of their times was such that a thousand years after they had ceased to exist as a sovereign people, their

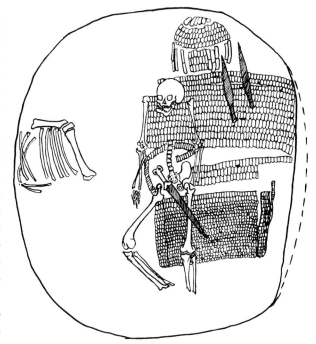

Sketch of the contents of a Scythian warrior's burial mound opened in the Nikolaev region. Dating from the 5th century BC, the tomb contains a complete suit of scale armour, including a helmet and leggings: cf. Plate D.

Comparative chronology of principal events in Scythian and Greek history

Scythians	Greeks	Scythians	Greeks
c.3200 BC Horse domesticated in southern Russia			**519 BC** Athens and Plataea defeat Thebes
c.1500 BC Steppes inhabited by semi-nomadic horse-breeding tribes		**c.514–512 BC** Scythians repel Persian invasion of south Russia under Darius the Great	**511 BC** Spartan campaign against Athens
Early 7th C. BC Cimmerian and Scythian conquest of Urartu; Scythian activity in Middle East recorded in Assyrian texts	**7th C. BC** Poetry of Hesiod	**c.496 BC** Scythian expedition to Chersonesus in Thrace	**Early 5th C. BC** Writings of Aeschylus
670s BC Scythian king Partatua fights Assyria, marries daughter of Assyrian ruler Esarhaddon	**c.664 BC** First recorded naval engagement, between corinth and Corcyra (Corfu)	**Late 490s BC** Scythians negotiate alliance against Persia with Spartan king Cleomenes I	**490 BC** Battle of Marathon **480 BC** Battles of Thermopylae and Salamis
Mid-7th C. BC King Madyes leads Scythian expedition to borders of Egypt		**Mid-5th C. BC** Reign of King Scyles	**c.450 BC** Herodotus visits trading colony at Olbia and records description Scythians
c.652–626 BC Period of Scythian influence in Media	**640s BC** Poetry of Archilochus; first minting of coins in Asia Minor **621 BC** Draconian laws in Athens	**c.350 BC** Beginning of Sarmatian expansion into Scythian territory **339 BC** Scytho-Macedonian war: King Atheas killed in battle with forces of Philip II in Rumania	**c.437 BC** Pericles sends expedition to Black Sea area **338 BC** Philip II defeats Athens and Thebes at Charonea
612 BC Medes and Scythians capture Nineveh and destroy Assyrian Empire **Late 7th C. BC** Medes drive Scythians north of Caucasus into north Pontic area		**330 BC** Alexander's general Zopyrion is routed by Scythians near Olbia **310–309 BC** Scythians defeat Caucasians at Thatis River	**323 BC** Death of Alexander the Great
Early 6th C. BC Scythian philosopher Anacharsis travels in Greece	**594 BC** Solonian laws in Athens	**c.200 BC** Scythians gradually withdraw into Crimea **110–106 BC** Scythians defeated in Crimea by King Mithridates Eupator of Pontus (Bosphoran kingdom)	

artland and the territories which they dominated far beyond it continued to be known as 'greater Scythia'.

From the very beginnings of their emergence on the world scene the Scythians took part in the greatest campaigns of their times, defeating such mighty contemporaries as Assyria, Urartu, Babylonia, Media and Persia.

The ancient Greek historian Herodotus recorded that Cimmerian tribes had inhabited the Black Sea steppes before the Scythians. Then came the Scythians, and conquered the Cimmerians. Pursued by the Scythians, Cimmerian nomads crossed the Caucasus and spread into the countries of western Asia; and the pursuing Scythians, led over the mountains by their king Madyes, defeated the Medes they found in their path.

Early in the 7th century the Scythians moved against Assyria. The official records of Assyria are highly selective, giving much space to Assyrian victories but remaining silent about Assyrian defeats. Fortunately, a more balanced picture can be built up by comparing various surviving sources—not only the official record, but also the reports of spies, and the questions put by Assyrian kings to oracles when seeking advice.

After a period of warfare between the Scythians and Assyrians the politically skilled Assyrian king Esarhaddon succeeded in winning peace with them, for a time, by the presentation of rich gifts, and by marrying off his daughter to the Scythian king Partatua. The Scythians' attentions were diverted towards Palestine and Egypt. A Biblical prophet referred to the Scythians as 'the ancient, mighty people whose language is hard to understand. They are always courageous, and their quivers are like an open grave. They will eat your harvest and bread, they will eat your sons and daughters, they will eat your sheep and oxen, they will eat your grapes and figs.' Only by paying heavy tribute did the Pharaoh Psammetichus I (reigned 663–609) save his country from Scythian invasion.

From Egypt the Scythians returned to Assyria, and in the period c. 650–620 BC Media, one of the richest states of the ancient East, fell steadily under their influence. In 612 BC a Scytho–Median army finally captured Nineveh and overthrew the Assyrian Empire.

Herodotus says of the Scythian dominance of Asia: 'The Scythians ravaged the whole of Asia. They not only took tribute from each people, but also made raids and pillaged everything these peoples had. Once Kiaksar and the Medians invited the Scythians to a feast, and killed them.' This suggests that the Scythian leadership were annihilated by treachery. At any event, the bulk of the nomad army drifted back north of the Caucasus at the end of the 7th century.

Much remains unclear, however, about the campaigns of the Scythians in the Middle East. It is not known whether they came south as disorganised nomad bands of plunderers, each following the tales of rich pickings which may have drifted back in the wake of the first bands to make the journey; or as a unified people with a disciplined 'state' army. We are also ignorant of the extent to which they returned to the Black Sea steppes, or remained in the Middle East.

Undoubtedly, they learned a lot from contact with the progressive civilisations of the Middle East. In the realm of warcraft, they learned how to fight effectively against cavalry and infantry alike, how to fight mounted and dismounted, and how to take well-fortified cities by storm. Bravery and a warlike nature alone would not have enabled them to defeat powerful and sophisticated ancient empires.

Of great importance, obviously, were the weapons and armour which enabled the warrior to strike down his enemy while protecting himself and his horse. The complex of Scythian war-gear was formed, by experience and by imitation, during their great campaigns in the Middle East; before this period the Scythians did not use defensive armour. Our knowledge of their weapons and armour comes from their funerary customs. Scythian dead were buried in barrow-mounds ('kurgans'), and the warrior was accompanied on his journey into eternity by the possessions which were most important to him in life. Rich finds of weapons and armour of many kinds have rewarded the excavation of Scythian barrows, including the tombs of many Scythian women. The grave of a common warrior usually contained a bow and several dozen arrows, and a pair of spears or a spear and a javelin. Royal tombs often yield whole arsenals of defensive armour, helmets, swords, quivers of arrows, dozens of spears, and—in the early period—large numbers of horse skeletons.

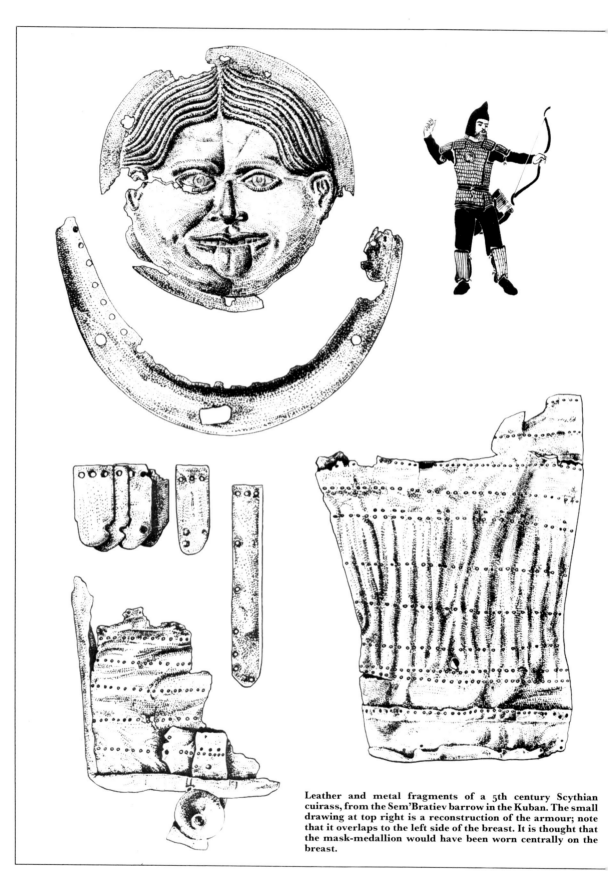

Leather and metal fragments of a 5th century Scythian cuirass, from the Sem'Bratiev barrow in the Kuban. The small drawing at top right is a reconstruction of the armour; note that it overlaps to the left side of the breast. It is thought that the mask-medallion would have been worn centrally on the breast.

Defensive Armour

exible leather corselets covered with small over-
pping scales of bronze or iron were worn in the
icient Middle East from about the middle of the
cond millenium before Christ. Quickly recognis-
g the advantage of a corselet proof against most
vord and spear-thrusts, the Scythians experimen-
d until they found the most efficient method of
ranging the overlapping 'fish-scales'. Remaining
use for thousands of years, the scale corselet ranks
a milestone in the development of the art of war
ongside the discovery and harnessing of bronze
d iron weapons, gunpowder and artillery.

The Scythians applied the same basic method to
her defensive armour. They covered helmets,
ields, girdles, and fabric clothing with small metal
ates, in contrast to the Middle Eastern smiths,
ho limited the use of scale to corselets. Scythian
mourers cut the scales from sheet metal with a
ointed tool or shears; several dozen were needed to
shion a long-sleeved corselet. They were attached
a soft leather base by thin leather thongs or
iimal tendons; each scale was set in such a way
at it covered one third or one half of the width of
e next scale sideways, and the row of plates
erlapped the one below it, protecting the stitch-
g where it was exposed in holes through the metal.
spear or arrow thus had to penetrate up to three
four basic scale thicknesses at most points on the
rface. Despite this excellent protection, the cor-
let did not greatly hinder the movements of the
ounted warrior; only ring-mail gave greater ease
manoeuvre.

These corselets, which gave the Scythian riders
otection from the earliest period of their military
eatness, varied in details of design. Some light-
eight types had metal scales only around the neck
d upper breast, or only on the front surface.
enerally the corselet resembled a short-sleeved
irt entirely covered with scales; we know of only a
w examples with long sleeves. The importance of
oulder protection in a mounted combat was
flected in many cases by the addition of a doubled
ke of scale-work across the upper back and
tending forward over the shoulders to the sides of
e breast. Ease of movement was preserved by
aking the corselet from different sizes of scales:

small plates were used at elbow and shoulder, so as
not to hinder arm movement, while the back and
abdomen were covered with fewer, larger plates. As
a rule the scales were of one metal only, usually iron;
but we know of examples of corselets with different
areas fashioned from iron and bronze: the spectacle
must have been magnificent, as polished bronze
glittered in the sun against the lustreless iron
background. Finds from royal and noble tombs
include corselets with each scale covered with fine
gold leaf, and bronze scales decorated with figures
of lions, deer, or elk heads.

The process of armour development was not
entirely straightforward, however; and helmets
provide us with an example of changing styles and
materials. In the 6th century BC Scythian warriors
wore heavy cast-bronze helmets, fitting tightly to
the skull and protecting it part way down the face
by means of cheek-pieces which left cut-outs for the
eyes, and giving good protection to the back of the
head. Many such helmets have been found in the
Northern Caucasus, particularly in the Kuban
area, where the most ancient graves have been
discovered. (We may speculate that noblemen who
took part in the Middle Eastern campaigns were
buried here.) This style is popularly termed the
'Kuban helmet'.

From the 5th century onwards helmets of scale
construction began to replace the 'Kuban' type.
The pointed leather ('Phrygian') caps or hoods,
commonplace among the Scythians, provided the
model: they were covered with overlapping metal
scales, and often had added cheek-pieces and neck-
guards, a nasal being the only important element
missing. Easy to make, they gave reliable protection
against sword cuts. These helmets were in quite
widespread use.

It was also in the 5th century that, among
Scythian noblemen, the Greek helmet began to be
worn; more than 60 bronze helmets made in Greece
have been found in the richer Scythian barrows.
These light, strong, beautiful pieces are generally of
Corinthian, Chalcidian or Attic type.

The use of Scythian leg defences, of leather
covered with metal plates, seems to have been at
least partly replaced during the 5th century by
Greek-style metal greaves. These may have been
limited to heavy cavalry only. The armoured
horseman of the 6th and early 5th centuries was

Part of an elaborately embossed Greek breastplate, from an armour discovered in a 4th century barrow in the Kuban. It is clear that there was much contact between the Scythians and the Greek communities on the northern Black Sea coast even before the rise of Macedon brought the two powers into confrontation.

characterised by iron-faced leggings; his successor of the late 5th and 4th century, by greaves worn over fabric trousers. Prosperous leaders sometimes had gilded greaves; and a superb pair found about 150 years ago and now in the Hermitage, Leningrad have Gorgon heads on the knee-pieces and pairs of snakes, tail down, worked down the sides. Our colour plates show some examples of Greek helmets and greaves, originally heavy infantry items, modified for use by Scythian heavy cavalry.

The Scythians placed importance on the shield and its decoration. While ordinary warriors seem to have used light shields of woven osiers—e.g. the example on the famous Solokha comb—the heavy

cavalry carried more massive shields faced wi[th] iron. The classic construction was a wooden ba[se] faced with scales of iron, sewn to each other and [to] the backing with wire. There is evidence of som[e] use, presumably by the richer nobles, of shield[s] completely faced with single, round iron plate[s] with applied decorative motifs of other metals. (It [is] thought that the scale-faced shields may also ha[ve] borne such decorations on occasion.) Two go[ld] decorative plates, more than 30cm long, were fou[nd] in the graves of early Scythian noblemen [at] Kostromskaya Stanistsa and Kelermes in th[e] Kuban; the former is in the shape of a deer, and th[e] latter, a panther, in the 'animal style' so typical [of] the Scythians. A bronze fish motif has also bee[n] found in a grave not far from the famous Tolstay[a] Mogila site, and a gold deer—showing strong Gree[k] influence—in the royal tomb at Kul Oba.

Another major category of Scythian defensi[ve]

8

9

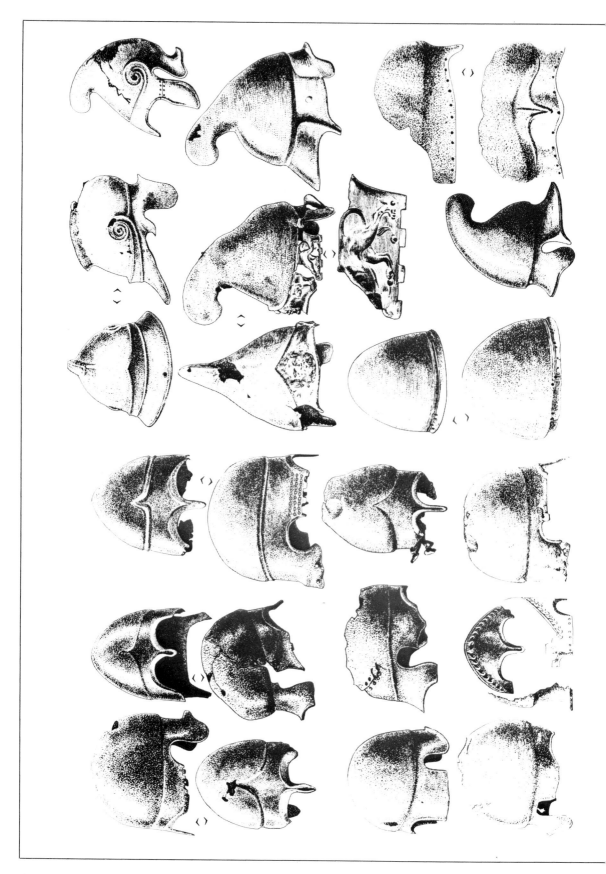

our is the girdle, of leather faced with strips of
, bronze, or even silver or gold. Typical of the
y period, and of dismounted warriors whose
omens were not protected by the neck of the
se, these broad girdles often had several rows of
es or strips. Narrow belts for the slinging of
rds, daggers, battleaxes, bows and quivers,
etstones and whips were also worn by the
thians. The defensive girdle declined in size with
passage of time, and was eventually 'absorbed'
the increasingly common corselet.

rotection for the horse took several forms. Since
6th century BC metal plates and pendant
orations on the bridle helped to protect the
se's head and cheeks. There is evidence to
port the use in some cases of a leather horse-cloth
attached metal scales, and a thick felt 'apron'
he breast, in which the enemy's arrows became
k without penetrating.

'Kuban'-type Scythian bronze helmet found in the 6th century
barrow at Kelermes (Stanitsa Kelermesskaya). See Plate A
for reconstruction. Note the holes for attachment of an
aventail; the raised ribs all round the lower edge and part way
round the back of the skull; the raised flange at the brow, and
the reinforcement running centrally over the skull to the point
between the eyes.

Offensive Weapons

long-range fighting the Scythians used bows
slings; at intermediate range they employed
rs and javelins; and for hand-to-hand combat,
rds, axes, maces, and daggers.

s and Arrows

ry Scythian had a bow and arrows; all male
ves contain great numbers of arrowheads, and so
bout one in three of all female graves, and many
dren's graves. Arrowheads are found in the
bs of king and humble rider alike. The bow and
ws accompanied the Scythian from cradle to
e, and beyond; it is clear that the Scythians
eved that the dead would need them to hunt
fight in the world beyond. Scythian ar-
heads can be found all over the Eurasian
pes, and the Scythian style of bow was in

k, Thracian and Macedonian helmets, and fragments of
ets, all recovered from Scythian burial mounds. More
60 have been found in Scythian burials, some in original
lition and some apparently modified by local smiths: see
e E. The three columns on the left are Attic, Chalcidian,
perhaps remains of Corinthian types; those on the right
Thracian, as favoured by the Macedonians—though note
resting Thracian/Boeotian composite.

widespread use throughout Eastern Europe and
Western and Central Asia.

Sadly, the materials used to make bows—wood,
bone and animal tendons—perish easily, and only a
few out of the 5,000 or so known Scythian graves
contain identifiable remains of bows, and those so
poorly preserved that it is almost impossible to
reconstruct their original appearance with confidence. Luckily we can also study sculptural
evidence, pictorial metalwork from grave finds, and
the descriptions of ancient authors.

Surviving written descriptions compare the un-
strung, recurved Scythian bow with the Greek letter
sigma (Σ), or the Black Sea coastline. Ammianus
Marcellinus wrote: 'While the bows of all peoples
are made of flexible branches, Scythian bows . . .
resemble the crescent moon, with both ends curved
inwards'. The middle of the bow is described as a
regular curve. This description corresponds well
with the bows depicted on gold and silver bowls
found in the graves of Scythian kings at Kul Oba
and Voronezh. Only the grips and ends of bows
have been preserved, the latter having decorative
bone tips in the graves of some noblemen. Judging
by pictures and the length of the arrows, the bow
was quite short—up to 80cm; but as with all
examples of the classic Eastern 'composite' bow, the

This helmet from the famous 4th century Solokha burial hoard seems to be of Greek manufacture—'Attic'-type?—with later modifications by Scythian armourers. Extra neck and cheek defences were sometimes added.

length of its cast was determined by its very taut compression rather than by its length of stave. Ancient authors write that the string was of horsehair or animal tendon.

The arrow shaft itself was of reed or a thin birch branch. The fletching was made conventionally from birds' feathers. The heads were of iron, bronze, or sometimes of bone. There were different types, apparently designed specifically for the hunt, or to pierce corselets, shields and helmets. The 'trilobate' arrowheads found in such numbers in the excavated tombs are of strict aerodynamic forms and superbly exact workmanship; the simplicity and perfection of their lines stands comparison with modern rockets.

The Scythian bow was capable of accuracy at considerable range. An old Greek grave found at Olbia, the ancient trading city on the Dniepr–Bug estuary, bears an inscription to the effect that Anaxagoras son of Dimagoras shot an arrow from his bow to a range of 282 *orgyiai* (521.6 metres). Since Olbians, like the inhabitants of other ancient cities on the Black Sea coast, favoured the Scythian bow, it is fair to assume that the archer achieved his feat with a weapon obtained from the steppe horsemen: a feat which is breathtaking even today.

Apparently, Scythians could match the rate of shooting recorded for skilled archers of the Middle Ages—between ten and 12 arrows a minute. The Scythian carried anything between 30 and 150 arrows into battle, and could expend them in three to 15 minutes' shooting. Given the hundreds of

mounted archers who took part in most enga[ge]ments, one can only imagine the hail of dea[dly] arrows which fell among their enemies. [The] penetrative force of the arrows was also consid[er]able. Some graves yield human skeletons w[ith] arrowheads embedded in the skull or spine t[o a] depth of two to three centimetres. Many picture[s on] ancient cups and vessels show warriors in corse[let] pierced by arrows, or hoplite shields simila[rly] penetrated. Many authors of antiquity wrote t[hat] Scythian arrowheads were poisoned.

The Scythian bow was extremely stiff a[nd] powerful, and great strength and skill were nee[ded] to string it. According to Herodotus, Heracles [left] his bow to his sons when he set out from Scyt[hia,] saying that only the son who could string it as he [did] would rule the Black Sea steppes. The youngest s[on,] Scythes, succeeded, and Herodotus wrote that [the] race of Scythians was descended from him. T[his] legend may explain why scenes showing [the] shooting of the bow, or the passing of a bow fr[om] one warrior to another, or the stringing of the b[ow,] occupy a prominent place in Scythian art.

The bow was carried in a special case slung fr[om] the belt on campaign, and was only removed [for] battle or the chase. In the pre-Scythian peri[od,] when the northern Black Sea steppes were [in]habited by the Cimmerians, a case of simple fo[rm] was used. The Scythian case, called by the Gre[eks] a *gorytos*, held both the bow and up to 75 arro[ws;] sadly, no complete example is known to survive[;] only rotten fragments of leather have been foun[d in] graves. We know, however, that its length was t[wo-]thirds that of the bow, and that the quiver sect[ion] had a metal-clasped cover. Early Scythian tom[bs] yield many bronze, bone, and even gold buckl[es.]

The quiver section was often covered with [an] ornate gold facing plate decorated with figure[s of] deer; but since the plate covered only a part of [the] gorytos, finds in early graves do not show us [the] complete form of the case in this period. Only in [the] 4th century BC did it become the fashion to face [the] whole gorytos with metal plates. The first find [of] this type was unearthed from the Chertomlyk r[oyal] tomb site. This large gold plate is covered with p[lant] motifs, animals, figures of men, women and ch[ild]ren in Greek clothing, items of furniture, weap[ons] and even architectural structures. For deca[des] opinions differed about the significance of th[ese]

strations; but it has now been established that
y represent scenes from the *Iliad* of Homer, in
rticular the visit of Achilles to the island of Skiros,
d the story of how this was discovered by
ysseus.

For nearly 50 years the Chertomlyk gorytos
nained unique; then, three more gold facings
re discovered, identical to the Chertomlyk
mple. It is apparent that a master metalsmith,
ssibly Greek, set up a workshop in one of the
thian centres, making a series of gold plates for
ering the gorytos to the order of Scythian kings
d nobles. Many must have been stolen from
ves and melted down; doubtless many more
nain in the ground, awaiting discovery.

Quite recently an interesting find was made
ich proves the existence of another series of gold
ytos used by prosperous leaders. A very rich
cedonian royal grave, which had somehow
aped plundering, was found at the site of a small
eek settlement called Vergina. Amongst other

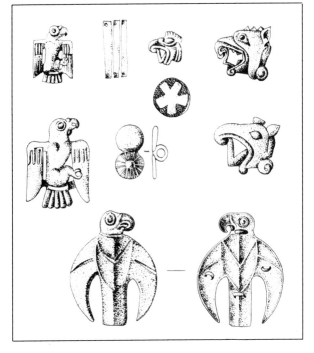

Various decorative plates and studs from Scythian belts, both
everyday and ceremonial, recovered from burial sites of the
6th to 4th centuries. The Scythian love of animal motifs, the so-
called 'feral' style of ornamentation, produced wonderfully
vigorous images which remind us of the similar but distinct
Scandinavian and Germanic styles of a thousand years later.

**o different Greek greaves recovered from barrows on the
ch peninsula. The beautiful workmanship of these exactly
portioned defences is obvious even from these simple
tches. The greaves split down the back centrally, and were
d to the calf purely by the spring of the thinly-beaten metal.
s not hard to see why the work of Greek armourers
ealed to the Scythian nobility.**

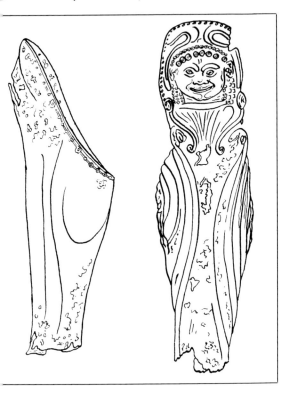

items the archaeologists unearthed the remains of a
gorytos which was identical to one found in a
Scythian mound in the Northern Caucasus nearly
100 years ago. The Scythians combined bowcase
and quiver was not used in Greece and Macedonia;
how could this undoubtedly Scythian gorytos have
found its way into the grave of a Macedonian
nobleman—perhaps even Philip II himself?

Shortly before this interment, negotiations took
place between Philip of Macedon and the king of
Scythia; they broke down without agreement being
reached, and war broke out between the Scythians
and Macedonians. In 339 BC the 90-year-old
Scythian king Atheas was killed in battle
with the Macedonians, who captured rich trophies.
Apparently the gorytos found in the Macedonian
grave was either part of the ritual exchange of gifts
at the time of negotiation, or war booty. This
example, and that from Karagodeuashkh in the
Northern Caucasus, have similar forms to the
Chertomlyk gorytos and to other finds from
Scythian barrows; both show the assault and
looting of a city, believed by scholars to be a
representation of the fall of Troy.

One of the most famous of all Scythian finds: the golden comb, featuring a battle scene, from the 4th century Solokha royal burial mound.

A very interesting gorytos was found shortly before the First World War in the Scythian royal burial of Solokha. Generally similar to those described above, it bears a scene of special interest. Unlike other examples decorated with traditional animal motifs, ornamented gold or silver plates, or scenes of Classical warfare, the Solokha find shows episodes from the life of the Scythians. The central part is filled with a scene of three young Scythians on foot fighting two elderly Scythians on horseback. On the left is a young warrior armed with a battleaxe, carrying a shield and with a gorytos on his belt, who attacks a mounted Scythian armed with a spear. This rider is hurrying to the aid of a comrade-in-arms who has been attacked, dragged from his horse, and killed by two young men before having a chance to draw his sword. The elderly horseman seems certain to suffer defeat. This scene calls to mind a story told by Herodotus.

He writes that Scythian warriors setting off on campaign to western Asia left their wives in Scythia, together with many slaves. 'These slaves and the

Scythian women gave birth to a younger generati of men, who determined to rise against the warri upon their return from Media. They dug a de moat from the Taurus Mountains [the Crime Mountains] to the Maeotic Lake [the Sea of Azo and when the returning warriors attempted to cr the moat the young men attacked them. The eld Scythians were at first unable to defeat them. Th one warrior exclaimed: "What are we doing? fighting against them we deplete both our o forces and the number of our slaves. Let us drop spears and bows and take up whips. Seeing weapon in hand, they imagined that they were equals, and of the same noble origins. But wh they see us with whips instead of weapons they understand that they are only our slaves, and v not be able to resist us". The Scythians followed t advice, and the slaves, astonished, forgot abo fighting and took flight. Thus the Scythia returned to their homes.'

Apparently, the Solokha gorytos shows an e sode from the early stages of the battle between veterans and the young men.

It is notable that although the use of the quiv for arrows alone, was very widespread in ancient Middle East, no single example among dozens of surviving sculptures and pictorial me objects showing Scythians includes a quiver; combined bow and arrow case is universal.

The sling seems also to have been a popu weapon among the Scythians, and many gra contain several dozen sling-stones—in one case, many as 75.

Swords and Daggers

The sword and dagger also play an important p in the culture of the Scythians. The ancient Gre traveller, historian and geographer Herodot whose notes taken during a visit to the Black S region in the 5th century remain our major writ source, wrote that 'Ares, the God of War, was only deity whom the Scythians worshipped and whom they built altars'. The war-god embodied fortune of war. Every region of Scythia had a la mound made of brushwood. 'An old iron sword v placed on top of each mound. That was an altar the God of War, to whom more sacrifices w offered than to any other god. Every year th brought cattle and horses to these swords. Fr long captured enemies they sacrificed every hundredth man. First a libation of wine was poured over their heads. Then they cut their victims' throats and collected the blood, and carried it to the top of the mound and poured it over the sword. At the foot of the altar they cut the right arm and shoulder from the body, and tossed them in the air, each arm being left to lie where it fell. The trunks lay separately.' Herodotus's story was confirmed by the archaeological excavations near Zaporozhye. It was hard for the Scythians to make the mounds of brushwood demanded by tradition, living as they did on the almost treeless steppes. Mounds of sand were raised instead; and it was one of these which was discovered near Zaporozhye, surrounded by grave-mounds dating back to the 4th century. The altar itself was at least a hundred years older, since the sword found at its top dates from the 5th century. The origins of the Scythian sword are still not entirely clear, but mounting material evidence points towards the weapons carried by their predecessors on the steppes, the Cimmerians. By

late in the 7th century the form of the Scythian sword was established. In its earliest examples it has a two-edged, almost parallel-sided blade tapering at the point, about 60–70cm long—though a single example of a huge sword with a blade one metre long, dated to the 6th century, has been found in the Crimea. Daggers, of similar shape, were generally 35–40cm long.

The most ancient finds come from the late 7th/early 6th century mounds at Melgunov and Kelermes. The two swords are very alike, differing only in secondary details: so much alike, indeed, that they may have been modelled on the same standard pattern, perhaps even in the same smithy. Each is decorated with thin gold plates fixed round

Detail from the Solokha comb: note the evident mixture of Greek and Scythian war-gear worn by the mounted warrior, who has a Corinthian helmet, and muscled greaves sprung over his Scythian trousers. The cuirass and girdle are Scythian. The crescent-shaped shield is a common image in Pontic art; the footsoldier who bears it wears highly decorated clothing, a sword interestingly and untypically slung on the left hip in the position normally occupied by the gorytos, and what seems to be the typical Scythian cap.

Detail from the Solokha comb: the shield is reconstructed Plate F.

Detail from the Solokha comb: the Greek linen cuirass, w added scale protection on the breast, tied-down shoulder yo and 'feathered' skirt, could hardly be clearer.

the hilt and scabbard, on which fine geometri patterns and animal forms are stamped. T animals are both real—deer, goats, lions—a mythical—various combinations of the goat, li bull, fish, and human archer. Both swords featur scene of winged gods standing around a sacred tr It is quite obvious that the ornamentation has uniformity of style. The craftsman's manner is quaint mixture of different styles from Urartu (present-day Armenia), Assyria and Media. Some the animal forms decorating the scabbards, e.g. t deer and mountain goat, were later to becom typical of Scythian art, however.

These swords were brought back by t Scythians from their conquests in the Middle Ea and Asia Minor. It is natural that local smith producing goods to the order of their Scythia

:upiers, should blend the artistic styles of different
ltures into a curious whole.

With the passage of time, the Scythian sword
anged shape. The 5th century saw the parallel-
ed blade replaced by an elongated isosceles
angle with a continuous taper down its whole
igth; and in the 4th century single-edged blades
peared beside the double-edged. During the
i century the pommel changed from a simple
issbar shape to a more complex fashion, with two
lons' of iron rising and curling inwards. In the
urse of the 4th century the pommel tended to
vert to a simpler oval shape; the grip, too,
anged, from a cylindrical to a double-tapered or
al shape much more convenient to the hand. The
ard took on a triangular shape, with a sharp,
rved indent in the centre of the bottom edge. The
:companying photographs illustrate these points
ire clearly than words.

The scabbard was made of wood covered with
ither, throughout Scythian history. It hung from
e belt by a thong passing through its projecting
ir', and various sculptural finds indicate that it
is worn well forward on the right side of the
domen. Some of our colour plates show how this
ght have worked in practice for a horseman.

A curious find was recently made in a grave-
ound at Belozerka near Zaporozhye, unlike
ything previously recorded by archaeologists.
ie tribesmen who were burying their comrade 23
nturies ago had made a deep, narrow hole in the
or of the barrow, and had inserted a sword into it
int downwards, the pommel being barely visible
love the floor-level. The sword was a 'dress' or
remonial one, its hilt and scabbard sheathed in
in gold plate. On the scabbard were illustrations
predatory animals clawing their prey—a popular
ythian motif. A lion and a griffon pounce on a
er; two panthers race alone, wiry and menacing.
n the protruding 'ear' of the scabbard is a superb
ad of a wild boar, the Greek letters 'πOP' cut in
forehead.

The interest lies not only in the curious method of
rial, but also in the fact that similar scenes are
und on the sword from the famous barrow of
ul Oba, excavated nearly 150 years ago on the
itskirts of Kerch. The ornamentation of the
ul Oba scabbard has much in common with the
:lozerka find; while the 'ears' have different

motifs, the main five-figured scenes are literally
identical, having been embossed into the plate with
the same stamp. (The Belozerka sword is shorter
than that from Kul Oba, which explains why some
scenes from the latter are missing from the former.)
This appears to be convincing proof of the existence
of armourers' shops on the north coast of the Black
Sea, probably in Panticapaeum or some other city
of the kingdom of Bosphorus, which then ran along
the coast of the strait and peninsula of Kerch.

Until recently it was thought that the great
majority of Scythian swords were short; but
increasing numbers of finds of longer blades have
changed our view of Scythian tactics, since long
swords would naturally allow a greater tactical
flexibility in the use of mounted men against both
infantry and cavalry.

Spears, Javelins and Axes

Many spears and javelins were used by the
Scythians, and one or two are found beside almost
every buried warrior. Some barrows contain much
greater numbers: more than ten were found in the
Scythian royal barrow near Berdyansk on the Sea of
Azov.

Until recently historians believed that the
Scythians used only short spears or javelins, which
could be either thrown or wielded in close combat;
this stemmed from the simple fact that Scythian
burial chambers are too short for a longer weapon.
That a spear might be broken before being laid in
the grave did not occur to anyone until attention
was drawn to the relationship of points and shafts as
they were found lying in a number of tombs. It has
now become clear that some of the Scythian spears
are more properly termed lances, since they were
more than three metres long and obviously intended for mounted combat.

Shorter spears, about 1.7–1.8 metres long, were
used both for throwing and for thrusting, and from
pictorial evidence on funerary finds in rich Scythian
burial mounds it is clear that they were used equally
for war and for the chase. Thrown by a trained
hand, such spears could kill or wound at ranges up
to 30 metres. Spearheads of both long and short
types come in various forms, usually leaf-shaped,
with a central spine for added strength and a socket
for the shaft. Length varies greatly, from 30 to
72cm, and the longer heads were presumably for

Decorative and defensive bridle fittings recovered from Scythian barrows of the 5th to 4th centuries BC.

sier penetration of armour. Ferrules from the butt ds of shafts have also been found.

Javelins intended solely for missile use, or 'darts', d heads of an entirely different form. They had a ig iron shank with a small pyramidal head, arply barbed, and were clearly designed to make aard to withdraw them from a wound or a pierced eld.

Nearly a hundred iron battleaxes of various types ve been found in the burial mounds excavated in mer Scythian territories. One magnificent speci-n was recovered from the famous Kelermes rrow, covered entirely with gold plate except for e narrow 'tomahawk' blade. The ornamentation mbines a number of styles. The blade has graved forms of mountain goats and deer; more ats adorn the head, and the gold-covered shaft esents a stunning pattern of mingled figures of al and mythical beasts, birds and insects.

Elegant maces with lobed heads served not only weapons but also as symbols of authority. A fine ecimen was found in the Solokha barrow. The companying photographs illustrate this and the

T:
e 6th century Kelermes mound yielded this shield dec-ation in the shape of a lioness or panther; and the deer came m the Kostromskaya burial. Of solid gold and more than :m long, these pieces are superb examples of the Scythian imal style.

other types of weapons described above.

To summarise, one can state with confidence that the range of high-quality weapons developed in Scythia's period of greatness covered the whole spectrum of pre-gunpowder armament, and equip-ped her warriors for every type of mounted and dismounted combat against every kind of enemy. Throughout the subsequent history of arms, only the sabre and the ring-mail body-armour represent types not already introduced and mastered by the Scythians—and there is even some evidence that they made use of ring-mail.

Most Scythian weapons and armour were made by native smiths, using great quantities of local or imported iron and bronze, and working them to a high standard of craftsmanship. For the richest members of Scythian society, magnificent cere-monial weapons were made by Greek armourers in the trading cities along the north Pontic coast, combining Scythian styles of decoration with Greek craftsmanship in silver and gold to produce genuine masterpieces of the metalsmith's art. Safe within the burial mounds of their owners, these richly dec-orated weapons, cuirasses and shields have sur-vived the ravages of the centuries to adorn the

19

world's finest museum collections. Scythian achievements in weaponry are thought to have had a considerable influence on the development of arms in neighbouring lands. The Greeks of the Pontic colonies adopted the full range of Scythian weapons in preference to their own, and Scythian-made weaponry has been found thousands of kilometres to the north, west and east of Scythia, as far as the Arctic Circle, Germany and Mongolia.

The Scythian Army

It is difficult to reconstruct the organisation of the Scythian army. Written sources confirm its division into cavalry and infantry, and this is not contradicted by archaeological data. Cavalry was the principle arm of the Scythians, as was typically the case among nomadic societies. Herodotus and Thucydides put it in a clear-cut way, stating that each Scythian warrior was a mounted archer. On the other hand, Diodorus Siculus wrote that in one particular battle the Scythians fielded twice as many foot as horse. This is not surprising, in fact; for Diodorus was dealing with events of the late 4th century, when the gradual transition from nomadic to sedentary life among the Scythians was becoming marked; and it should also be noted that the majority of the combatants in the battle he describes were drawn from areas where this process was especially advanced.

Throughout early Scythian history the overwhelming majority of the men were mounted; infantry consisted of the poorer Scythians, and levies from those settled tribes whose territory was now dominated by the Scythians. Commoners from these vassal tribes, which were obliged to provide military service, served on foot, and their more well-to-do leaders in the cavalry.

The bulk of the cavalry was probably made up of lightly-armed warriors, protected by no more than fur or hide jackets and headgear. The shock force of the Scythian host was the professional, heavily-armed cavalry commanded by local princes. Both horses and riders were well protected. They fought in formation, under discipline, and brought to the battlefield considerable experience of warfare. The

engagement opened with a shower of arrows a sling-stones, followed at closer range by darts a javelins. The heavy cavalry then charged in cl formation, delivering the main blow on the centre the enemy's array. They were certainly capable manoeuvre in battle, breaking through the ene ranks, regrouping in the thick of the action, a changing direction to strike at the right place at right time. When the enemy had been broken lightly-armed mass of the Scythian horse closed to finish them off.

Almost the whole of the adult population Scythia, including a large number of the wome folk, fought on campaign. It is impossible estimate the numbers of soldiers Scythia could into the field simultaneously; Scythian kings the selves wished that they knew. Herodotus tells us King Ariantes, who attempted to establish t numbers of his subjects by ordering every Scythia on pain of death, to bring one arrowhead to t muster. So many arrowheads were brought that decided to have a monument made of them. bronze vessel cast from the melted-down metal w reputed to contain 600 *amphorae*, with walls fingers thick; at the standard Attic measure, t represents 23,400 litres (5,200 gallons).

Thucydides wrote that the Scythian army w larger than a 150,000-strong Thracian tribal ho

A gold decorative plaque showing Scythian archers, from 4th century Kul Oba burial. Note fur-trimmed jackets, corated trousers, and short boots. The top-knot hairstyle Plate B) is unusual in Scythian pictorial work. The sh sharply recurved bows are accentuated here.

Bronze Scythian arrowheads from a 4th century burial near Kiev. Note the long single barb on three of these pieces.

d that not one people in Europe or Asia could ist the Scythians unaided, if the Scythians were l of one will'. This comment draws attention to e traditional nature of nomadic tribal societies, hose strength is normally fairly widely dispersed in ore or less independent groups, and which can dom if ever bring their whole strength into the ld together. Against this, one must remember at Scythia was a military state, whose entire social ucture was geared to the needs of war; one might rrow the words of the mighty Persian king arius the Great about the Persian nation, d term the Scythians 'a people at arms'.

The Persian Invasion

ore than a hundred years had passed since the ythians returned to the steppes north of the Black a and the Caucasus from their conquests in the liddle East. All veterans of those campaigns were ng dead of their wounds or old age, and laid to rest der their grassy barrows; but in the fortresses and wns of Armenia, Syria, Palestine, and even abylon, the terrible memories of their war-cries d their whistling arrows were still green. In ythia, old warriors recounted their grandfathers' orious feats of arms in faraway lands to the young

bloods gathered round them. In an oral society the names of kings and the exact order of events would fade gently into legend; but the legend would live on.

But now the half-forgotten past threatened to strike back, and dark clouds gathered over the broad plains of Scythia. In more than one hundred years of her vigour she had invaded many neighbouring lands; now, it seemed, Scythia would pay in her turn. A formidable enemy was preparing to invade the Pontic steppes, claiming justification in the wars of long ago. The enemy was none other than the Great King of Persia, Darius I Hystaspes of the Achaemenid dynasty.

Towards the end of the 6th century BC Darius I had managed to create a mighty state, the most powerful nation on earth at that time. His empire stretched from Egypt to India. Preparing for future conquests, he increased his power by introducing a number of reforms, and created a strong army. Since the Greek city-states stood in his path westwards, they would be conquered. But before he could move against them the empire's northern marches must be made safe from possible new inroads by the nomads of the steppes—the Scythians, and their neighbours the Sauromatae. We owe most of what we know of the events which

This magnificent gold vessel from the Kul Oba royal tomb shows many details of Scythian costume. This warrior is stringing his bow, bracing it behind his knee; note the typical pointed cap or hood, long jacket with fur or fleece trimming at the edges, decorated trousers, and short boots tied at t ankle. The hair seems normally to have been worn long a loose, and beards were apparently worn by all adult men

lowed to Herodotus and to other ancient Greek
[a]d Roman authors.

Before invading Scythia the Persians carried out
[r]econnaissance in force. Ariaramnes, the ruler of
[on]e of the satrapies, led northwards a fleet of 100
[sh]ips; he landed on the Scythian coast and probed
[in]land, taking many prisoners—among them,
[bl]ood-brothers of the Scythian king. This evidence
[of] Darius's warlike intentions was soon confirmed.
[H]erodotus tells us that he sent messengers to his
[va]ssal states, with orders to contribute levies to the
[ar]my and the fleet, and to build a bridge across the
[H]ellespont, which was known as the Thracian
[B]osphorus at this period. Within a relatively short
[ti]me he mustered forces estimated by Herodotus at
[70]0,000 men, and by other authors at the even more
[fa]ntastic figure of 800,000. The real number was
[ce]rtainly much smaller, as was the number of
[sh]ips—600, if one is to believe Herodotus. Never-
[th]eless, though we cannot venture an estimate of
[ou]r own, this was certainly one of the greatest
[ar]mies of antiquity.

Crossing the bridge of boats over the Hellespont,
this enormous force broke through the resistance of
the Thracian tribes without difficulty. By the spring
or summer of 512 BC Darius had reached the
Danube, which was also bridged by anchoring ships
across its span. The mighty army of invasion began
to roll across to the left bank of the river onto
Scythian territory. Initially Darius planned to
destroy the bridge behind him, adding the ships'
crews and the bridge guard to the bulk of his army;
but his advisers persuaded him to leave it intact.
Instead, writes Herodotus, he took a leather thong
and tied 60 knots in it, and gave it to the
commanders of the rearguard. He ordered them to
untie one knot each day after the army had
marched. If he did not return by the time all the
knots were untied, the rearguard was to sail for
home; but until that day came they were to guard
the bridge at all costs.

The Scythians were well aware of the menace
which threatened them, and knew that they could
not defeat such an overwhelmingly superior force in

[A]nother face of the Kul Oba vessel shows two warriors
[c]onversing, both holding spears or javelins. The gorytos is
[cl]early indicated on the left hip of the bare-headed spearman;
[h]is companion's shield is interesting, perhaps representing a
[p]lain leather covering over a wooden or wicker base.

[R]IGHT:
[T]his third view of the Kul Oba vessel shows a warrior, his
[g]orytos exposed to us, binding a wounded comrade's leg.

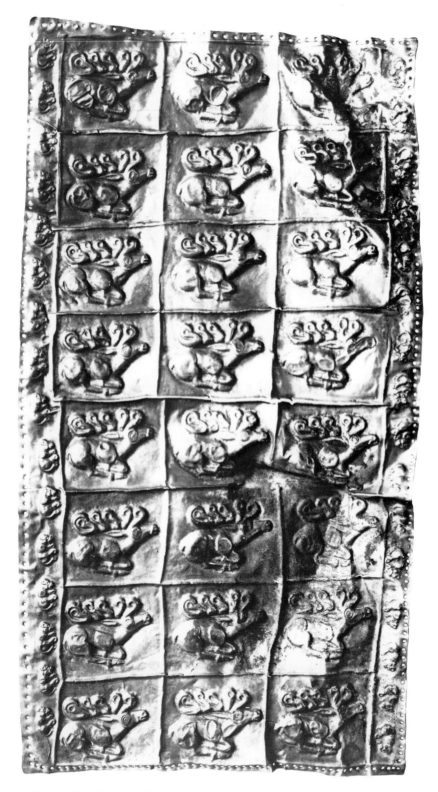

Gold gorytos facing plate from the 6th century Kelermes barrow, with a repeat pattern of deer motifs in the Scythian style. At this period only part of the gorytos was faced with decorative plates, and the disintegration of the leather structure leaves us with only an imperfect idea of the overall shape.

1: Scythian king, early 6th C. BC
2: Urartian nobleman, early 6th C. BC

A

1: Scythian warrior, late 6th/early 5th C. BC
2: Scythian warrior, 4th C. BC
3: Thracian warrior, 4th C. BC

B

1: Scythian warrior, 5th C. BC
2: Scythian nobleman, 4th C. BC

C

1: Armoured warrior, 5th C. BC
2: Armoured warrior, late 5th/early 4th C. BC

D

1: Scythian king, late 5th/early 4th C. BC
2: Armoured nobleman, 4th C. BC

E

1: Sindo-Meothic nobleman, 5th C. BC
2: Scythian nobleman, 5th C. BC
3: Scythian noblewoman, 4th C. BC

F

1: Scythian king, 4th C. BC
2: Scythian queen and prince, 4th C. BC
3: Royal bodyguard, 4th C. BC

G

1: Young Scythian warrior, 4th C. BC
2: Scythian king, 4th C. BC
3: Nobleman, 4th C. BC

en battle, or at least, not unaided. The council of ⌐ders turned to neighbouring tribes for help, ⌐nding out messengers to spread word of the ⌐nger, and to point out that the Persians would not ⌐ content with conquering Scythia alone. But their ⌐ighbours' opinions were divided, and most re-⌐sed to form an alliance. They justified this by ⌐inting out that the Persians were apparently ⌐sponding in kind to the Scythian invasions of the ⌐evious century. They declined to make enemies ⌐ the Persians in such a cause, though determined ⌐ defend themselves if the invaders proved to have ⌐ider ambitions than punishing the Scythians.

Since even those forces which were promised to ⌐em would arrive too late to form a united front ⌐ainst the rapidly advancing Persians, the ⌐ythians had no choice but to fight on their own. ⌐t this time Scythia was divided into three separate ⌐ngdoms; the largest tribe provided the supreme ⌐ler, King Idanthyrsus, and his subordinate kings ⌐re named Scopasis and Taxacis. Each led the ⌐st of his own tribe. At a council of war they agreed ⌐at it would be madness to oppose such a superior ⌐my in open battle, and that they must play for ⌐ne, hoping to wear the Persians out and forcing ⌐em to react to their strategy. They started to

withdraw in the face of the invader, filling up wells and springs and burning off the grass as they went. The women, children and old people trekked north, driving the herds with them. Only the warriors and young women—who fought as equals—remained on the steppe.

The host was divided in two. The more mobile part, led by King Scopasis, was to head for the Danube to meet the invaders half way. They were to avoid direct contact, and to move east, keeping a day's march (perhaps 30 or 35 kilometres) ahead of the Persians, scorching the grazing and driving off the game as they went. The bulk of the Scythian army, led by Idanthyrsus and consisting of his own and Taxacis's troops, was to retreat parallel to the Persians and on their northern flank. Their two-fold task was to keep the enemy from turning towards the northern refuge of their people, and to channel the Persians always towards the burnt-out, water-less plains. The Scythians' goal was to let the enemy wear himself out on an exhausting pursuit-march

Gold facing plate for a gorytos recovered from the 4th century royal burial at Chertomlyk. The decoration, in the Classical style, shows an incident from Homer's 'Iliad': the visit of Achilles to the Isle of Skyros. Produced by a Greek craftsman to Scythian order, this piece has a border frieze of beasts and monsters of the kind found on so many surviving artefacts.

The world-famous gold pectoral found in the royal burial at Tolstaya Mogila, dating from the 4th century, is reconstructed on our Plate G. This is an enlarged detail from the pectoral, showing two Scythians—their bows and arrows always close at hand—apparently dressing a fleece.

across the steppes, and to attack him if a good opportunity arose.

We know from Herodotus that the Persian invasion force was mostly infantry, with some cavalry and a considerable train of baggage. The Scythians were all mounted, until perhaps the last stages of the campaign when footsoldiers of neighbouring peoples came to their aid. The weapons of the two sides were similar; the Scythians were probably the better archers, given their reputation as the finest bowmen of their time, and this gave them an obvious advantage in exactly the kind of running fight which they planned.

The Persians began their long march eastwards into the Scythian heartland. Their progress was slow. Historians and archaeologists have not agreed as to what route they followed, or how far they finally penetrated. Our principal source is not of great help on this point: Herodotus writes that the Scythians fell back through the territories of the tribes which had refused to help them, hoping to

involve them in the war, thus implying th the Persians covered about 5,000 kilometres in on 60 days. This is clearly impossible, and the advanc of a basically infantry army over such a distanc would have taken three or four times as long even a forced pace. There were several major riv barriers—the Dniestr, Southern Bug, Ingul, I gulets, Dniepr, Don, and many smaller river Besides the problems of terrain, the Persians we constantly in danger—and towards the end of the march, the very present danger—of harassin attacks, and were short of food, water and forag

The Scythians kept falling back, refusing to gi battle. By the time they reached the steppes north the Sea of Azov, the leather thong left with th commander of the Danube bridge guard had lo one third of its knots. There seemed to the Persia to be no end to the campaign, and its goals were far out of reach as ever. Not only were the Scythia undefeated; they grew stronger every day, as the fell back towards new forces joining them from th east. They had everything the invaders lacked food, water and forage.

At last Darius decided to halt, and build a larg fortified camp on the northern coast of the Sea

ov somewhere in the vicinity of the modern town
Berdyansk. His purpose is not clear. He might
ve planned to leave a strong garrison to pin down
e enemy in that area while the mass of his army
ntinued east; or he might have intended to wait
his fleet to bring up provisions by sea. In any
ent, the construction of the camp was never
ished. Its walls were only half-built when Darius
lled out for some reason, and resumed his pursuit
the Scythians. Although the decisive battle he
ved still eluded him, he had already lost a
nsiderable number of men in skirmishes. It was
en that Darius did something he had never done
fore. He sent a messenger to King Idanthyrsus.
'Strange man', he said, 'why do you continually
n away, when given the choice? If you think
urself strong enough to contend with me, then
p roaming, and turn and fight. If you confess
urself to be weaker than I, you will have to stop
yway, and open negotiations with your ruler,
nging him earth and water as symbols of
bmission'.
Herodotus reports that Idanthyrsus replied in
these words: 'I have never run away for fear of any
man. I am wandering, as I always wander in time of
peace. You ask why I did not fight you at once. May
I remind you that we have neither cities nor
cultivated land of our own; since we are not afraid of
our territory being ruined and plundered, we had
no reason to fight you outright . . . Not will we, until
we see fit. Instead of earth and water, I will send you
other gifts, of the kind you deserve; and you will pay
me dearly for calling yourself my ruler'.

Idanthyrsus kept his promise. The Scythians now
began to adopt more aggressive tactics, harrassing
and waylaying Persian foraging parties. The
Scythian horsemen dominated the Persians in these
skirmishes, sending Persian cavalry fleeing back in
disorder into the ranks of their own infantry.
Idanthyrsus had now committed the bulk of his
personal forces, and detached Scopasis's horsemen
westwards on an important mission. Since they had

**Gorytos facing plate recently discovered in the Macedonian
royal tomb—alleged by some to be that of Philip II—near the
site of Vergina, northern Greece. This 4th century relic bears
decoration which is believed to depict the fall of Troy.**

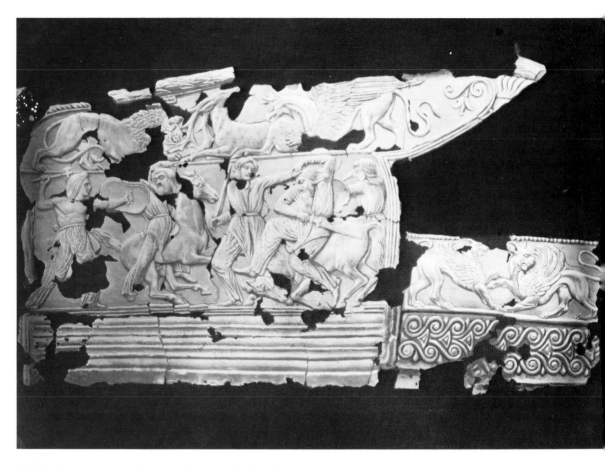

Gilded silver gorytos facing plate from the Solokha burial, showing a battle between young and old Scythian warriors; the legendary allusion is discussed in the text.

now begun to believe that the enemy could be defeated, the Scythians determined to cut them off by destroying the Danube boat-bridge. Scopasis reached the Danube, and parleyed with the Greek vassal force who guarded the bridge. It is reported that he accepted an assurance that the Greeks would dismantle the bridge, but rode eastwards again without waiting to see it done, and that the Greeks broke their word and kept the bridge intact.

Now Idanthyrsus sent Darius the gifts he had promised: strange gifts for the great king—a mouse, a frog, a bird, and five arrows. Darius chose to interpret these as meaning that the Scythians accepted unconditional surrender: they were offering him their land (for mice live in the earth and eat grain, like men); their water (for frogs live in water); their horses (represented by the bird, symbolising the means of their freedom and their most valuable possession); and were laying down their arms before him (the arrows). A courtier

interpreted the message in a different way, howeve[r] 'If you Persians do not fly away like the birds, [or] hide in the earth like mice, or leap into a lake li[ke] frogs, then you will never see your homes again, b[ut] will die under our arrows.' The continuing course [of] the campaign soon convinced Darius that t[he] second interpretation was the right one.

One day he received word that the enemy seem[ed] about to offer him the decisive battle upon which h[is] hopes rested. Even though his army was weaken[ed] and tired out, he was still confident in its ability [to] overwhelm the Scythians in pitched battle. T[he] adversaries ranged themselves for combat—but [it] soon transpired that far from seeking battle, t[he] Scythians had thought of a new way to show the[ir] disregard for the great king. As the armies faced o[ne] another, a frightened hare started up from the gra[ss] between the battle lines—and the Scythians hors[e-] men whirled away to pursue it. The message w[as] unmistakable to the Persians: 'These people hold [us] in utter contempt.' Darius decided, at long last, [to] salvage his army while he could still escape from t[he] boundless steppes of Scythia.

One night fires were banked high in his camp; the
[wou]nded and those unable to travel fast were left
[beh]ind, with the tale that the army was going out to
[giv]e the Scythians to battle. But instead Darius led
[a fo]rced march back towards the Danube, aban-
[don]ing his wounded and all his train in an attempt
[to r]each the bridge while he still could.

[A] second Scythian attempt to persuade the
[Gre]eks to destroy the bridge seemed to have
[suc]ceeded, but it was only a feint; the bridge was
[onl]y opened by the distance of a bow-shot. The
[Per]sians and Scythians missed one another in the
[dar]kness of night, and the next morning Darius
[fou]nd with relief that his means of escape was still
[int]act. He led his surviving forces into safety,
[lea]ving a large number dead on the steppes without
[eve]r having come to battle.

[T]he victory over Darius brought the Scythians a
[rep]utation for invincibility, which is confirmed in
[ma]ny Greek and Roman accounts.

Scythian Warcraft

[An]cient sources offer us only the most scarce and
[gen]eral information on the conduct of war by the
[Scy]thians. Even less is known about the turbulent
[5th] century than about the Persian invasion. One
[thi]ng is clear, however; the Scythians expanded
[the]ir influence westwards and north-westwards. A
[sig]n of this is the famous cache of arms found near
[Vet]taszkowo in Poland; these are probably the
[gra]ve-goods of a leader killed in the assault on a
[for]tress there, and laid to rest with a panoply of
[wh]ich a sword, a golden fish decoration from a
[shi]eld, and richly decorated horse-trappings sur-
[viv]e.

[A] little more is known about Scythian campaigns
[aga]inst the Thracians. After Darius was driven
[bac]k with shame, the Scythians started to press
[the]ir western neighbours, and continued to do
[so] throughout the 5th and 4th centuries BC. The
[eve]nts of the second half of the 4th century are the
[mo]st interesting; it was at this time that Macedonia
[beg]an to grow strong under the leadership of Philip
[II.] Thrace found herself between the devil and the
[dee]p blue sea: on her west, Macedonia, and beyond
[the] Danube, Scythia. The high king of the

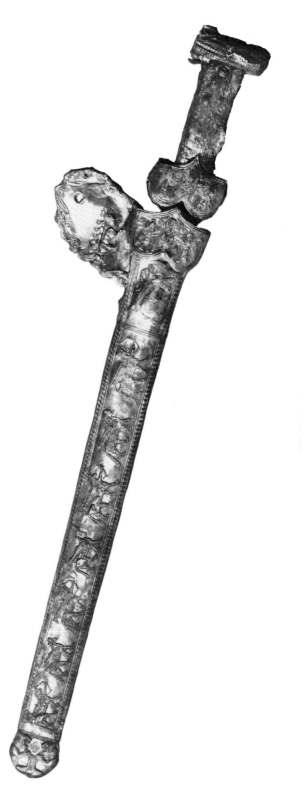

The highly ornamented sword, its hilt and scabbard faced
with stamped gold plate, found in the 6th century Kelermes
burial; this is one of the two oldest Scythian swords known.
Note the straight-sided grip and simple crossbar pommel. The
protruding 'ear' is pierced for the slinging thong.

Scythians, the aged and cunning Atheas, had long wished to add the lands of the Thracians to his range. The long diplomatic struggle for influence in Thrace ended in 339 BC when the 90-year-old king was killed and his army defeated by the Macedonians.

Yet this defeat, though bitter, could not have ruined Scythian power. Only nine years later Zopyrion, a general sent by Alexander the Great, invaded Scythia with 30,000 men with the goal of conquering Scythia's ally Olbia. He met with utter defeat, and his army left its bones on the steppes near Olbia. To our frustration, no details have come

down to us of the course of these two battles or tactics used.

The only more or less detailed account of battle fought by the Scythians comes to us fr Diodorus Siculus, who describes events on Scyth eastern borders in the late 4th century BC. 310–309 BC Scythia took a part in the confl between heirs of ther Bosphoran king, Paerisad The throne went to the king's eldest son Satyr but his brother Eumeles contested the cla Fleeing from the capital, Panticapaeum, he t refuge with the Thataeans who lived along Kuban River in the Northern Caucasus. T

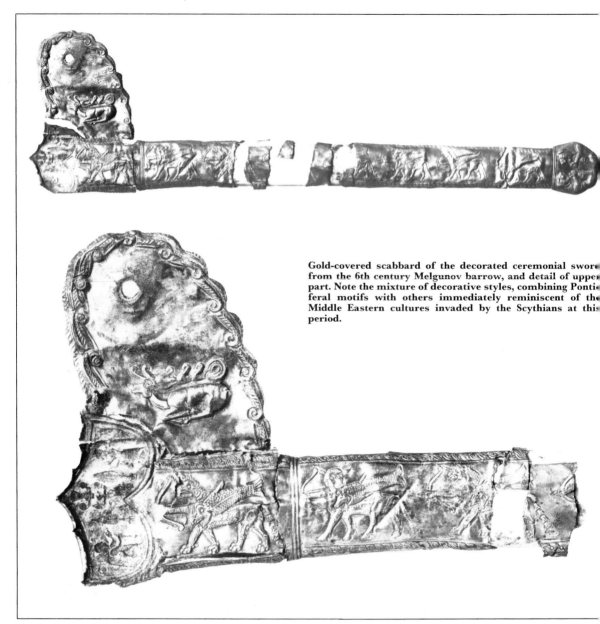

Gold-covered scabbard of the decorated ceremonial swor from the 6th century Melgunov barrow, and detail of uppe part. Note the mixture of decorative styles, combining Ponti feral motifs with others immediately reminiscent of th Middle Eastern cultures invaded by the Scythians at thi period.

hataeans had been made vassals of the Bosphoran ngdom not long before, and seized this opportunity to free themselves. They sided with Eumeles, d their king, Aripharnes, led a large army of ,000 horse and 20,000 foot to resist the pursuing rces of Satyrus.

Satyrus had an impressive army himself, with ,000 Greek and as many Thracian mercenaries; it likely that the Greeks were equipped as hoplites, d that the Thracians were lightly-armed peltasts. e bulk of the Bosphoran army, however, was ade up of Scythians—10,000 horse and 20,000 ot—since Scythia had long maintained ties with e kingdom of Bosphorus. Note the ratio of horse foot in the opposing armies; in Satyrus's force, 1 2, and in the Thataean army, 1 to 1. No other my of Classical antiquity is recorded as having ch numbers of cavalry; even Alexander the Great, no paid great attention to his mounted arm, never lded more than 1 to 5 or 6 cavalry to infantry. his high cavalry content, at times exceeding the fantry, characterised the armies of northern ntic peoples in the Scythian period.

Satyrus fielded a total of 34,000 men and umeles and the Thataeans 42,000; apart from his erall superiority, the pretender had 20,000 horse the Scythians' 10,000. From what we know it ems that the weaponry of each side was largely entical, though archers were probably more umerous among the Scythians.

The Scythians marched up-country into the hataeans' territory, and were obliged by the lack forage to take with them a train of several undred wagons. When they reached the River hatis they found the enemy drawn up on the far nk to receive them. Satyrus made a bold decision: succeeded in crossing the river, made a fortified mp out of his wagon train, and drew up his troops mediately in front of it. He stationed Greek ercenaries, presumably in their usual phalanx rmation, on his right flank, supporting that wing th Thracian peltasts and a troop of Scythian orse. Another detachment of the cavalry and fantry held the left wing. In the centre Satyrus led s select shock-troops: the bulk of the Scythian orse, including the heavily-armoured élite.

Diodorus has little to tell us about the Thataean der of battle. On the whole it was similar to that of e enemy: Eumeles was on the left flank with a

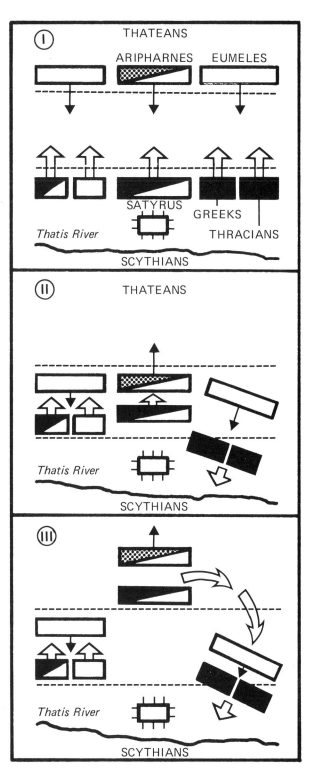

The battle of the River Thatis, 310 or 309 BC. (I) The armies ranged for battle. (II) Satyrus leads the Scythian heavy horse in a successful charge on the Thataean centre, while his right wing gives way before the enemy cavalry led by Eumeles. (III) After putting the enemy centre to flight, the Scythian horse regroups and swings round to take the Thataean left wing in the rear.

force of cavalry to engage the Greek and Thracian mercenaries, and infantry faced infantry on both wings. Aripharnes was in the centre with the bulk of his cavalry, headed by heavy units.

Both sides suffered heavy losses as soon as the battle began. At first Eumeles enjoyed some success on the left flank, and the Greeks and Thracians wavered. In the centre the Bosphoran king led his Scythian horse forward, smashing Aripharnes's cavalry in a short meeting engagement; they penetrated the enemy's second line, and soon put them to flight. The final blow was delivered by Satyrus leading the Scythians in a charge into the rear of Eumeles's command, ending his temporary advantage on the left wing and routing his forces. The surviving Thataean troops fled, and took refuge in a fortress.

This battle underlines the high combatant value of Scythian horse, achieved by firm discipline and the indisputable authority of its leaders as much as by the individual skills of the warriors. The Scythian cavalry managed to retain its cohesion after breaking through the enemy lines; regrouped in the thick of the battle; and decided the day by a second charge in another direction at a second body of the enemy. Very few armies of antiquity were capable of that manoeuvre.

The 4th century BC marked the peak of Scythian prestige, and the beginning of a steady decline. Gradually the Sarmatian tribes, who were related to the Scythians, began to cross the Don and encroach upon their territory. The Scythian range shrank, year by year, for reasons which are lost to us. For some time they lingered in 'Scythia Minor'—the area of the lower Dniepr and the Crimea. They yielded the northern Pontic steppes to the Sarmatians; and two hundred years after their victory on the Phatis River they disappeared altogether as a significant force in history. They leave us the mystery of their rise and their fall; and a haunting legacy of superb metalwork, chased with vigorous and beautiful images from the days of their barbaric splendour.

The Plates

Commentary by Dr. M. V. Gorelik

A1: Scythian king, early 6th century BC

This reconstruction of a Scythian king late in tʜ period of the Middle Eastern invasion is based ᴄ finds in the barrows near Kelermes in tʜ Kuban; the shield was found in a barrow neᴀ Stanitsa Kostromskaya. The king's iron axᴇ and the hilt and scabbard of his sword, have goʟ sheathing, chased in the Scythian style by Urartiᴀ (Armenian) craftsmen. He is also armed with ᴀ spear, and a bow and arrows in a goryt (combined bow and arrow case) decorated with ᴀ chased gold face plate; the gold clasp is probably Greek workmanship from Asia Minor. The caᴘ bronze helmet is of Scythian origin; the boᴅ armour, of iron scales sewn to leather, is typicalʟ Scythian. The iron facing of the shield is unique: the centre is a panther motif in Scythian 'animᴀ style'. From the girdle, decorated with gold ornᴀ ments, is slung a golden sup. The gold decoration bridle and breast-strap is Scythian work; the sadᴅ cloth, of a type common to all Iranian peoples, ᴀ typical of the Scythians.

A2: Urartian nobleman

These weapons and armour are based on finds froᴍ the excavation of the Urartian fortress ᴀ Teishebaini. The helmet is typical of this cultuʀ the armour is of bronze scale construction. ʜ carries a chased bronze quiver, and an iron swoʀ with ivory hilt decoration. His clothing is recoᴀ structed from wall-paintings and ceramics froᴍ Urartu.

B1: Scythian warrior, late 6th/early 5th century BC

Reconstructed from finds in barrow no. 3 neᴀ Khutor Popovka in Poltava province. The weaᴘ ons are an iron sword, a battle-axe and a spear. Tʜ body-girdle, from the barrow near the village ᴏ Shchuchinka, is very wide, and is made froᴍ several rows of iron scales and long curved platᴇ sewn to leather. The facing of the shield is uniquᴇ thick plates of bone are sewn to a wooden backinɢ Note the scalps of enemies decorating the bridʟ and a fresh scalp slung at the waist—after Her

complete contrast, a very plain and functional iron sword h a bronze hilt, the pommel shaped into two 'talons'. This s found in a Scythian burial dated to the 5th century, in the epr area.

...us. The saddle cloth is the flayed skin of a dead ...my.

: Scythian warrior, 4th century BC
...is prosperous warrior is reconstructed from finds ...barrow no. 493 near the village of Ilyintsi in ...nnitsa province. The leather armour has a ...ctoral and appliqué plates of bronze. The sword ...t is made of small bronze strips; the greaves are ... work of a Greek master. Weapons include a bow ...d arrows, a javelin and a spear. The fur or fleece ...ic is from pictorial work on the pectoral from ...lstaya Mogila barrow; the hairstyle, untypical of ... Scythians, is taken from representations on gold plates from Kul Oba barrow. He stands over his fallen Thracian enemy; it is believed that scalps were still taken at this time.

B3: Thracian warrior, 4th century BC
The costume is reconstructed from Greek vase-paintings and from Thracian metalwork objects; the weapons are from archaeological finds, and include the *kopis* or *machaira* sword, typical of this region and period. Note fox-fur cap, long ornamental cloak, and boots trimmed with goat's hair.

C1: Scythian warrior, 5th century BC
A rich warrior, reconstructed from finds at barrow no. 2 near the village of Volkovtsi in Poltava province. The leather body armour with attached scales resembles that worn by a warrior on the famous comb from the Solokha barrow. The typical shield has iron strips sewn to each other and to the wooden base with wire, and is edged with leather. Again, the girdle is of very narrow bronze strips. Note the length of the sword. He also carries a bow and arrows in a gorytos, a spear, a dagger and a javelin. The clothing comes from the pictorial decoration of the cup from Gaimanova Mogila barrow. The bridle was found complete in the tomb.

C2: Scythian nobleman, 4th century BC
This *nomarchos* or 'prince' is reconstructed from finds in barrow no. 1 near the village of Volkovtsi. The helmet is of Greek 'Attic' style. Bronze scales from the breast armour and bone scales from the shoulder-pieces were found in the tomb; the body defences are completed by a girdle of bronze plates. The warrior had a pointed iron axe, its haft decorated with a spiral gold band; a spear, a javelin, and a bow and arrows. The gorytos was decorated with gold plates, and others were sewn to the sleeves of the tunic. The gold-decorated bridle was found almost complete; the breast-strap of the harness had bronze decorative plates.

D1: Fully-armoured warrior, 5th century BC
Reconstructed from archaeological data from barrow no. 3 near Staikin Verkh in the forest-steppe zone (Northern Ukraine). The heavy armour, made of iron scales sewn to leather, gave an excellent defensive covering to the whole torso, the

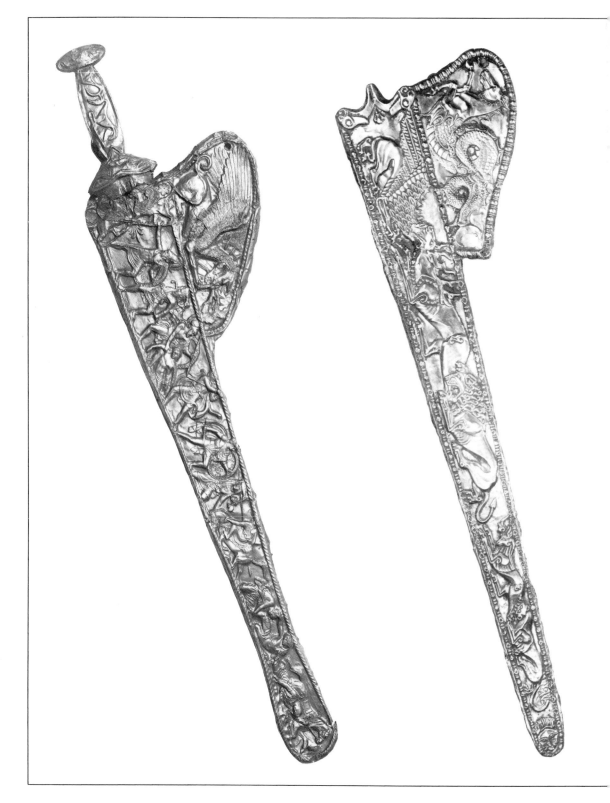

4th century ceremonial sword, the hilt and scabbard gold-plated; note the oval pommel and tapering grip more typical of this period. The decoration combines Scythian animal motifs with a battle scene in the Classical style including figures in both Greek and Scythian costume.

This ceremonial scabbard from the Kul Oba royal buria decorated entirely with real and mythical beasts; compare pure feral style of the animals near the tip, with the Greek-looking execution of the 'sea-horse' on the protrud 'ear'.

ns and the legs. We take the shield from the
okha comb, the Kul Oba vase, and other
rces. A comprehensive set of weapons is carried:
ord, battle-axe, spear, and bow and arrows.

: Fully-armoured warrior, late 5th/early 4th century BC
hough believed to be a rank-and-file fighting
n, this warrior reconstructed from finds in the
rrow near Novorozanovka village wears a beauti-
iron scale body armour of Scythian workman-
p, which was found almost intact. The helmet
s the form of a cap, with scales covering the skull
d iron strips on the ear-flaps and neck-guard.
te the usual bronze-strip girdle. The leggings
ach to bronze buttons, fixed to the inner surface
the body armour, by means of special loops. A
ically comprehensive set of weapons is carried.

: Scythian king, late 5th/early 4th century BC
constructed from finds in the Solokha barrow,
s warrior-king wears full battle armour. The
met is a re-worked Greek piece, of Attic,
alcidian or Corinthian manufacture. The body
nour is of iron scale construction, with short
eves. Note the Greek bronze greaves, which have
upper part cut off—perhaps in order to make it
ier to control the horse with the knees. The shield
ered with iron strips is taken from the Solokha
mb. Note the cup, of Greek workmanship in a
ythian decorative style, slung from the girdle.
e sword hilt and scabbard are covered with
ded silver plate, decorated by Greek craftsmen
h a battle-scene of Scythians, beasts and griffons.
e bronze mace thrust into the bronze-strip girdle
s a sign of the highest social rank as well as a
apon. The set of golden bridle decorations is
remely rich, with many frontal and nasal
urines; usually we find only a single figurine. The
of bronze decorations on the breast-strap of the
rness is typically Scythian. All harness dec-
tions were of Scythian workmanship, rather
n foreign. The front edge of the soft saddle has
pliqué golden triangles, and decorative gold
tes are sewn to the clothing and footwear. The
que is the work of a Greek master. Note also the
de bracelets, another mark of royal status.

: Fully-armoured Scythian nobleman, 4th century BC
constructed from the pictorial detail on the

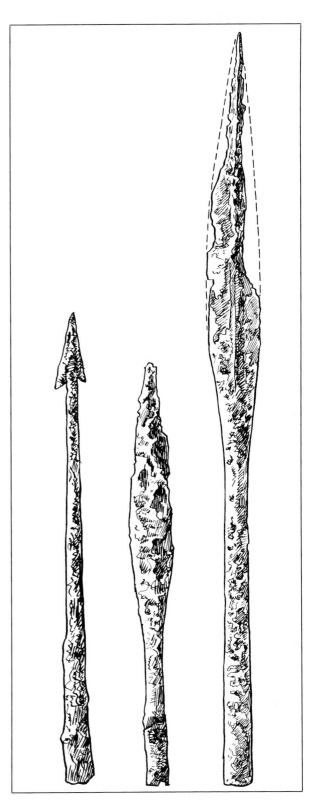

Scythian dart, javelin and spear heads, as they came from the
ground; the longest is more than 70cm from socket to tip. The
dart invites immediate comparison with the later Roman
pilum, and Frankish *angon*. These were unearthed from various
6th to 4th century burials.

Side view, and head detail, of the gold-sheathed axe from the 6th century mound at Kelermes. The exposed iron blade, now deteriorated, was decorated in the same style as the goldwork.

golden plate, of Scythian workmanship, found in Geremesov barrow. The bronze helmet of Chalcidian style, manufactured in Italy, has had a scale neckguard added by local smiths. The heavy scale body armour of local workmanship, with long sleeves and thigh defences, is supplemented by a triangular pectoral—we have not yet found one of these pieces, but we may see it depicted on later Sarmatian finds. The greaves have been deliberately modified, the knee-pieces being cut off and replaced by separate domed defences: a logical modification of heavy infantry armour for mounted use. The same sources show us a unique example of

scale breast armour for the horse. The shield, fac with iron strips and mounted with a bronze figur a fish, was found in a barrow near Ordzhonikidz Dniepropetrovsk province. The gorytos is fac with a superbly chased golden plate depicting eagle, worked by Greek craftsmen to Scyth order; this was found in Dört Oba barrow in Crimea.

F1: Sindo-Maeotic noblemen in full armour, 5th cent BC

This impressive figure is reconstructed from a sta now in Krasnodar Museum. The bronze helm manufactured in northern Italy, was found ne Stanitsa Dakhovskaya in the Kuban, close to site where the statue was found. The scale-fac shield is taken from the Solokha comb, and from

ent find in Kherson province. The leather body
[ar]mour had pauldrons and long sleeves; note that
[the] skirt is much longer at the rear than at the front.
[Th]e pauldrons and upper breast are decorated with
[lar]ge bronze plates in the animal style, which
[pro]bably combine defensive, aesthetic and magical
[fun]ctions. We have archaeological evidence for the
[use] of iron strips sewn to the sleeves. The breast and
[par]t of the armour are covered with iron scales. The
[stat]ue shows us clear representations of a long
[swo]rd, and a dagger in a tasselled sheath; one can
[als]o see a whip with two tassels, and a gorytos
[con]taining arrows and two bows.

Scythian nobleman, 5th century BC
[Th]e defensive armour was found in the tombs of the
[tow]n of Nymphaeum in the Crimea—the helmet in
[bar]row no. 1, the remainder in barrow no. 6—and
[is n]ow in the Ashmolean Museum, Oxford. The
[imp]orted bronze helmet of Illyrian style was re-
[wor]ked by a Scythian armourer, who cut off the
[nec]k-guard and attached it at the brow to form a
[pea]k. Part of a shoulder-piece of Classical-style
[leat]her armour, with attached bronze scales, was
[fou]nd in one tomb. The body armour was dec-
[ora]ted with a bronze plate in the form of an elk's
[hea]d on the breast. The girdle consisted of 'dagged'
[bro]nze strips. The Scythian greaves are of typical
[con]struction: strips of bronze are attached together
[and] to the leather base with wire. The sword, whose
[hil]ted hilt and sheath combined Scythian and
[Gre]ek decorative elements, was found in Ostraya
[Mo]gila barrow near the village of Tomakovka. The
[fin]e golden decorative work on the quiver-section of
[a] gorytos, and the truncated cone of gold which
[see]ms to be a decorative fixture for scalps, were
[fou]nd in the Crimea in a barrow near Ilyitchëvo.

Scythian noblewoman, 4th century BC
[Th]e women's tombs found near Ordzhonikidze
[yiel]ded several examples of war-gear for women
[war]riors. There was no body armour; the costume
[com]bined female elements—a 'tiara' headpiece,
[and] a collarless tunic with a long skirt—with male
[tro]users. Typical features were a bow and arrows in
[a g]orytos which had a sheath for a knife let into the
[fac]e, a spear and a javelin. Swords are rare in female
[tom]bs, only three being known. A mirror, as shown
[her]e slung to the girdle, is invariably found.

Two angles of the head, and one of the butt, of the bronze mace found in the 4th century royal tomb known as the Solokha mound.

G: Scythian king and his retinue on the march, 4th century BC

The costume of the king, G1, his queen and their little son, G2, are reconstructed from archaeological finds in the royal barrow of Tolstaya Mogila near Ordzhonikidze. The king wears an iron scale corselet with shoulder-pieces, the edges rimmed with gold, and the breast decorated with a chevron of stamped leather painted red and covered with gold foil. An iron Scythian girdle and bronze Greek greaves complete the defensive armour. The mace, once again, signifies the highest social rank. The sword, with chased gold decoration, is the work of Greek masters following Scythian designs. The silver plate facing the gorytos has appliqué decorations of gilded bronze in the Scythian animal style. The handle of the whip has a spiral gold band, and a tassel of gold beads at the head. The costume is lavishly decorated with gold plates, and on the king's breast can be seen the world-famous pectoral, the work of a Greek goldsmith.

The queen wears a gown, shawl and headdress decorated with the same kind of gold appliqué-work; the position of these plates in the tomb enabled archaeologists to reconstruct the form of the costume. Note the mirror slung at the waist. The little prince already wore a torque at the neck and a royal bracelet on his arm.

The king's mount has a bridle decorated with chased plates of gilded silver, of Greek workmanship, and a breast-strap with typically Scythian bronze ornaments.

The king's bodyguard ride with him, under a standard consisting of horsetails flying from a bronze capital mounted on a pole. The nobleman, G3, wears an armour found in a barrow near Dniepropetrovsk; his silver-decorated bridle, and the breast strap with a protective apron of bronze plates, come from Krasny Kut barrow. A field camp of Scythian travelling vans can be seen in the background.

H1: Young Scythian warrior, 4th century BC
A young warrior of humble birth brings the head of his first-slain enemy to his king, and is rewarded with a ritual cup of wine. He is armed with the usual bow and arrows in a gorytos. He has the head of a Macedonian military leader in his hand, and has stripped his enemy of his armour and weapons; a

5th century Scythian sculpture of a warrior king. Th[ese] ancient figures, which were originally raised on the top of finished burial mounds, have been found on several site[s]

eco-Macedonian helmet and greaves were d in a hoard near Oloneshti in Moldavia, a ld in Kurdzhipsky barrow in the Kuban, and ments of a sword at Olbia. Note the warrior's ᶃ hair—this could only be cut after he had killed first enemy.

Scythian king, 4th century BC
chief of one of the tribes that acknowledged the ᴉority of the Bosphoran kingdom, he is recon-ᴄted from finds at the Kul Oba royal barrow on Kerch peninsula in the Crimea. A number of ᴉron scales of the body armour were gilded; the le was of gilded iron strips, and Greek greaves ᴘlete the armour. Note the rich golden dec-ive work on the headgear and clothing; the

torque, bracelets and rings, all of Greek workman-ship; the hilt and sheath of the sword covered in Greek goldwork, and the knife and whetstone set in gold. The shield, of wood and leather, is decorated with a golden deer—again, Greek work made to Scythian order.

H3: Young nobleman, 4th century BC
This royal bodyguard of high birth has an armour of Graeco-Scythian type, combining bronze scales and strips, which seems to be the work of Bosphoran armourers. This kind of Scythian 'splinted' greaves were found in barrow no. 4 of the 'Seven Brothers' group in the Kuban. The sword is taken from one found in a barrow at Bolshaya Belozerka near Zaporoshye.

hian coin bearing the name and likeness of King Atai— ᴏusly, 'Ateas' or 'Atheas' in the Greek form—who died in le against the Macedonians at the age of 90. It is ᴀcteristic that he should be shown on horseback, bow in l. The Scythians attached enormous importance to the e herds upon which their culture was founded. It is ved that there were three main types of horse. The est, with a height to the withers of about 144 to 150cm (14¼ ¾ hands) was relatively scarce, and is mainly represented ery rich burials; it can be compared to an Arab oughbred, and was apparently used as a battle charger by

the nobility. The most frequent type was smaller, about 140cm (13¾hh) to the withers; this was an all-purpose breed for battle, work, and draught, and was rather smaller and lighter than our present-day saddle horse. The smallest, about 130cm (12¾hh) to the withers, was bred largely for its meat—a favourite Scythian dish. Pictorial sources suggest that the Scythians preferred to ride stallions. Mummified horses found at Pazyryk, and some cases of well-preserved horse burials on the European steppes, suggest that the preferred colour was 'red', and it seems that horses with white markings were bred out.

Notes sur les planches en couleurs

Toutes les planches sont fondées sur des découvertes archéologiques en Union Soviétique. Voir les légendes en langue anglaise pour les localités des tumulus applicables dans chaque cas.

A1 Casque en bronze et corselet en fer, à écailles monté sur cuir, de confection typiquement scythe. Noter le gorytos caractéristique: carquois et gaine à arc combinés—et la coupe pendue à la ceinture. **A2** Noble arménien, reconstitué d'après des fresques des ruines de Urartu, et des témoignages archéologiques.

B1 Remarquer la large ceinture protégeant l'abdomen; les scalps des ennemis à la bride et à la ceinture, et la peau écorchée d'un ennemi abattu utilisée comme couverture de cheval. Le bouclier est unique en son genre, garni de bandes en os. **B2** L'armure en cuir renforcée de plaques de bronze appliquées est scythe, mais les jambières sont grecques. Style de coiffure inhabituel, extrait d'images sur objets d'art en métal trouvé à Kul'Oba. Il s'agit d'un chef fortuné. **B3** Costume thracien reconstitué à partir de témoignages pictoraux sur des vases, etc.

C1 Riche guerrier portant une armure en cuir renforcée d'écailles et un bouclier en bois à bandes de fer. La longue épée n'est pas typique. **C2** Ce prince porte un casque grec Attic, des vêtements ornés de plaques d'or, et une armure à renfort en os sur les épaules, particularité peu ordinaire. Le gorytos, comme d'habitude, comporte des plaquettes en or sur la surface extérieure, décoré dans le style 'de chasse' des Scythes.

D1 Armure en écailles de fer complète, peu commune; noter la panoplie typiquement riche: épée, hache, javelot, arc et flèches. **D2** Une autre découverte archéologique admirable nous a permis de reconstituer cette armure en écailles complète; les jambières sont accrochées à des boutons en bronze à l'intérieur des basques de la tunique. Le casque en forme de casquette est renforcé d'écailles et de bandes de métal montées sur cuir.

E1 Roi guerrier en tenue de bataille complète: casque grec remanié, jambières grecques, harnais de cheval exceptionnellement très décoré, bouclier et corselet du type scythe, et armes et équipements superbement décorés par des artisans grecs mais dans le style scythe. Les bracelets, et la masse d'armes passée dans la ceinture, sont des attributs de royauté. **E2** L'un des gardes du corps nobles du roi; ici aussi, le casque et les jambières, de fabrication grecque, ont été modifiés par des artisans scythes. La protection pectorale du cheval par armure en écailles est unique en son genre. Le gorytos, découvert en Crimée, est de qualité particulièrement fine; une fois de plus, le style est scythe mais le travail est grec.

F1 Noter l'armure en cuir exceptionnelle, peinte et dorée; le casque de fabrication italienne, découvert dans le Kuban; le fouet garni de glands, et le gorytos avec deux arcs. **F2** Des objets découverts en Crimée, mais se trouvant actuellement en Angleterre, sont notamment: casque illyrien à protège-nuque découpé et refixé à l'avant, comme visière, par un armurier scythe. Ici, les jambières sont typiquement scythes. **F3** Les articles servant à la guerre sont rares mais pas inconnus dans les tombeaux des femmes, mais en pareil cas, des épées n'ont presque jamais été découvertes. Des pièces typiques sont le gorytos à fourreau de couteau incorporé à la plaque frontale et le miroir pendu à la ceinture, à la façon dont les hommes portaient parfois leurs coupes.

G Magnifiques costumes royaux d'un roi, de sa reine et de leur petit garçon, découverts dans des tombeaux royaux près d'Ordzhonikidze. L'ensemble comprend des éléments de travail local—décoration à motifs de chasse, et plaquettes d'or cousues sur les vêtements—il faut signaler aussi la contribution de maîtres-artisans grecs. L'ornement pectoral du roi est célèbre dans le monde entier en tant que découverte tombale. Derrière la famille royale se tient un garde-du-corps avec un étendard à queue de cheval.

H Un jeune guerrier d'humble naissance apporte comme tribut au roi la tête de son premier ennemi abattu: un officier macédonien. Il reçoit en récompense une coupe de vin rituelle. Le roi et son garde du corps noble portent divers articles d'origine mixte scythe et grecque. Des accessoires guerriers macédoniens capturés figurent parmi plusieurs précieuses découvertes.

Farbtafeln

Alle Rekonstruktionen basieren auf Funden in der Sowjetunion; Sieh Tafelbeschreibungen in englischer Sprache für Namen und Lage der jewe Grabhügel.

A1 Bronzehelm und eiserner Schuppenbrustpanzer (mit Lederunterlag typischer skythischer Ausführung; beachte den charakteristischen Goryt (binierter Bogen- und Pfeilköcher) soie die vom Gürtel hängende Trinksca Uratäischer Vornehmer, rekonstruiert nach Wandmalereien in den Ruine urartäischen Festung Tejsebaini und archäologischen Funden.

B1 Beachte den breiten Kampfgurt, der den Unterleib schützt, Skalp Feinden am Zaumzeug und Gürtel und die abgezogene Haut eines getö Feindes als Pferdedecke sowie den einmalige Schutzschild (mit Knochenp besetzt). **B2** Die Lederrüstung mit aufgesetzten Bronzeplatten ist skythisc Beinschienen jedoch griechisch. Ungewöhnlicher Haarstil, nach Bilder Metalplättchen von Kul Oba. Dies ist ein wohlhabender Krieger Thrakischer Krieger, rekonstruiert nach griechischer Vasenmalerei un chäologischen Funden.

C1 Reicher Krieger, Lederrüstung mit aufgesetzten Schuppen tragend un einem typischen hölzernen Schutzschild mit aufgesetzten eisernen Platter lange Schwert ist weniger typisch. **C2** Dieser Fürst trägt einen attischen l mit Goldplatten verzierte Kleidung und eine Rüstung mit ungewöhn Schulterverstärkung aus Knochenschuppen. Der Goryt hat, wie bei Vorne üblich, eine Goldplatte auf der Aussenfläche, im skythischen Tierstil ver:

D1 Ungewöhnlich kompletter Fund einer eisernen Schuppenrüstung, beachte den typisch reichhaltige Bewaffnung—Schwert, Axt, Lanze, Boge Pfeile. **D2** Ein anderer hervorragender archäologischer Fund ermöglicht c diese volle Schuppenrüstung zu rekonstruieren; die Beinschutz ist in Brc nöpfe an der Innenseite des Panzerhemdes eingehakt. Der Helm ist in phrygische Mütze geformt, mit auf Leder montierten Schuppen und Eise sen als Ohren- und Nackenschutz.

E1 Ein König in voller Kampfausrüstung, einschliesslich eines umgearbe griechischen Helmes, griechischem Beinschutz, einem ungewöhnlich reich verziertem Pferdegeschirr, einem Schild und Kampfgurt von skythischem Waffen und Ausrüstung hervorragend verziert von griechischen Handwe jedoch in skythischen Stil. Die goldenen Armreifen und der im Gürtel stec Streitkolben sind Zeichen des königlichen Rangs. **E2** Vollgerüsteter skyth Fürst; wiederum sind Helm und Beinschienen aus griechischer Herstellu skythischen Handwerken modifiziert worden. Der schuppengepanzerte Br chutz für das Pferd ist ein einmaliger Fund. Der Goryt, auf Krim gefunden, i besonders hoher Qualität; wiederum ist der Stil skythisch, jedoch die Ausfü griechisch.

F1 Beachte die ungewöhnliche Lederrüstung, schuppenbesetzt und verzi Italien hergestellter Helm, im Kubangebiet gefunden; eine mit Qu geschmückte Peitsche; und ein Goryt mit zwei Bögen. **F2** Funde von der nunmehr in England, schliessen einen illyrischen Helm mit abgeschnitt Nackenschutzein, der vorne als Schirm von einem skythischen Waffensc wieder angebracht wurde. Die Beinschienen sind typisch skythisch. Skythische Kriegsausrüstung in Frauengräbern ist ungewöhnlich, jedoch nicht unbel obwohl Schwerter in solchen Fällen sehr selten gefunden werden. Typisc Goryt, hier mit einer eingebauten Messerscheide an der Frontplatte, und Spiegel am Gurt in der Art und Weise, wie Männer manchmal Trinksc trugen.

G Herausragende Ausstattung eines Königs, seiner Königin und deren kl Sohn, nach Königsgräbern in der Nähe von Ordzhonikidze. Die Aussta beinhaltet sowohl einheimische Arbeit—Tierstil-Verzierung und auf die dung aufgenähte Goldplättchen—als auch Auftragsarbeit von griechi Meistern. Der Brustschmuck (pektorale) des Königs ist ein weltberü Grabfund. Hinter der königlichen Familie ist seine Leibwache mit Pferdeschwanzstandarte.

H Einer junger Krieger von niedriger Herkunft bringt der Kopf seines erste ihm getöteten Feindes—ein mazedonischer Offizier—zu seinem König und mit einem feierlichen Becher Weines belohnt. Der König und seine vorr Leibwache tragen zahlreiche Gegenstände gemischten skythisch-griechi Ursprungs. Erbeutete mazedonische Waffen (wie hier abgebildet) wurc verschiedenen skythischen Horten und Gräbern gefunden.